Birds in an African National Park

RENNIE BERE

ANDRE DEUTSCH

FIRST PUBLISHED 1969 BY
ANDRE DEUTSCH LIMITED
105 GREAT RUSSELL STREET
LONDON WC1
COPYRIGHT © 1969 BY RENNIE BERE
ALL RIGHTS RESERVED
PRINTED IN GREAT BRITAIN BY
EBENEZER BAYLIS AND SON LTD
THE TRINITY PRESS
WORCESTER AND LONDON
233 96127 5

By the same author

Wild Animals in an African National Park (*André Deutsch*)
The African Elephant (*Arthur Barker & Golden Press – New York*)
The Way to the Mountains of the Moon (*Arthur Barker*)
The Wild Mammals of Uganda (*Longmans*)

Birds in an African National Park

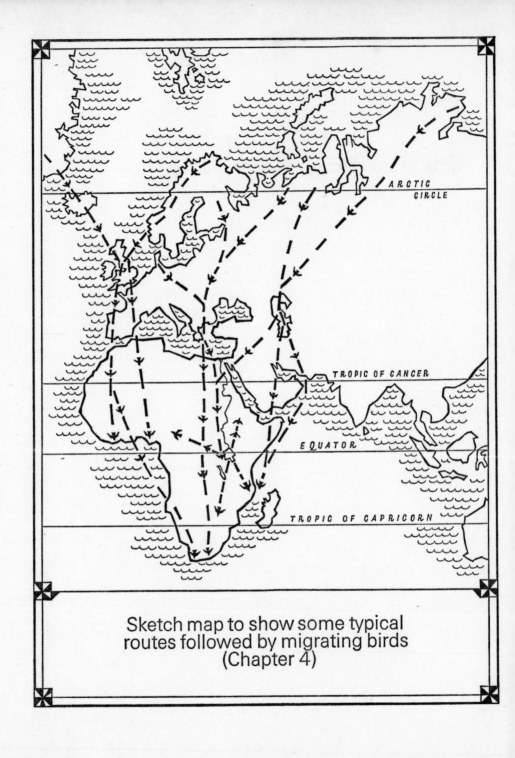

Sketch map to show some typical
routes followed by migrating birds
(Chapter 4)

for

WINWOOD
who has helped me to
understand the wildlife
of my own country

Author's Note

This book is about the birds of the two great National Parks in western Uganda, the Queen Elizabeth and Murchison Falls National Parks, which may reasonably be considered as two parts of the same ornithological area. Birds of the newer Kidepo Valley National Park, which is in a different part of the country, are not discussed. The approach is ecological; that is to say that I have described the birds against the background of the environment in which they live. I have also written about the habits of these birds and emphasized some of the more interesting aspects of their behaviour. The book is intended primarily for young readers, so I have included some brief general remarks about bird behaviour for the benefit of those who are unfamiliar with the ways of birds. More experienced readers may safely skip these few paragraphs: for example, the account of breeding and nesting on pages 9–11. I have avoided the use of scientific names in the text but have listed these at the end. This list shows all species mentioned in the text together with a few others. It is not a full check list of the birds of the region.

I have referred constantly to several books on East African birds as well as to some more general works of reference. The more important of these are listed in a short 'Reading and Reference List'. I have also made use of the handbook and reports of the Uganda National Parks, and to various relevant articles particularly Leslie Brown's *Observations on East African Birds of Prey* in Volume 1 of *East African Wildlife Journal*, 1963; several papers by Charles Pitman (in the *Bulletin of the British Ornithologists*

Club and in *Uganda Wildlife and Sport*); and a paper by Dr W. J. Eggeling in *The Uganda Journal* on the recovery of ringed birds in Uganda. I am grateful to the British Trust for Ornithology for information on this subject. I am grateful also to Winwood Reade and Bill Robinson for much good advice, and to Pamela Royds for her helpful editing.

Bude   RENNIE BERE
Cornwall
March 1969

Contents

Endpaper and frontispiece maps by Sheila Dorrell

Illustrations

ACKNOWLEDGEMENTS

The author wishes to thank Jeffrey Taylor for permission to reproduce the photographs facing pages 16, 48, 64, 81, 96, 129 and the lower of the two photographs facing pages 32 and 97; Roger Wheater for the photograph facing page 128, the upper of the two photographs facing pages 17, 32, 80 and the Black-headed Heron opposite page 112; John Savidge for the photographs facing page 49, the lower of the two photographs facing pages 17 and 80 and for the Skimmers and the Sacred Ibis opposite page 33; and Leslie Brown for the lower photograph opposite page 112 and for both photographs opposite page 113. The author is indebted to J. B. & S. Bottomley for both photographs facing page 65, the Wheatear opposite page 97 and the Kingfisher opposite page 112; and to Bill Robinson for the Whale-headed Stork opposite page 33.

1

The Background

Many years ago, before there was any idea of creating National Parks in Uganda, I was camping near Lake Albert with some friends. I was living and working in Uganda at the time but, although deeply interested in all forms of wildlife, I was not then a Game Warden. My friends and I had the use of an old life-boat, and our idea was to cross the lake, travel up the Nile as far as the Murchison Falls and return to our camp in one long day. We set off in the middle of the night and had some difficulty, in the dark, in finding our way through the great papyrus swamp which guards the mouth of the Nile. Eventually, however, we emerged on to the open river just as it was getting light. Birds of many kinds were flighting and calling as we cooked our breakfast on the boat; crocodiles were leaving the water after their night's fishing; hippopotamuses were returning to it after spending the hours of darkness grazing on land.

We saw a single bull elephant drinking in the shallows, but we did not expect to see the big herds until we were much further up-stream. Then we saw a superb old buffalo bull, standing on the bank, and steered in his direction. We stopped the boat, but the buffalo immediately moved out of sight. We started the engine again, but found that we were firmly stuck on a sandbank which we had failed to notice in our concentration upon the buffalo.

Two of us waded ashore but returned in an undignified hurry after almost bumping into the buffalo, which had gone no further than a nearby thicket. So we just sat hopefully on board expecting the strong current to move the boat. But nothing happened. There was only one thing to do, and we all got into the water to push, crocodiles notwithstanding. This worked; and eventually the boat swung free. The delay meant, however, that we had no chance of reaching the Falls. But we had had a wonderful opportunity of watching the superb bird life of the river while we were marooned on the sandbank. We were in the middle of an area magnificently rich in birds; and I recollect particularly an eagle swooping down upon the water and flying away with a duckling in its talons.

No part of the world excepting South America can compare with tropical Africa for large and conspicuously coloured birds. No part of tropical Africa is richer in bird life than the great lakes and rivers in the heart of the continent. When the Uganda National Parks were started in 1952, they included some of the best bird country on earth. Two and a half years later I was appointed Chief Warden of these Parks and had all these marvellous birds among my charges.

Over five hundred species of bird have been seen in Uganda's two great National Parks. This figure is more than the total recorded for Britain, although the area is not much larger than the English county of Somerset. The Parks lie at the heart of the lakes region of Africa. Lakes Edward and George, with a hundred miles of shore-line, form part of the Queen Elizabeth National Park. The River Nile flows through the Murchison Falls National Park for over ninety miles. The lakes and the river are richly stocked with fish which provide abundant food for a wonderful collection of water birds. Many of these, including pelicans and cormorants, live almost entirely on fish.

The lake-shores and the banks of the Nile are very varied. There are small sandy beaches, marshes and papyrus swamps. In places there are steep banks and low sand-stone cliffs. Elsewhere, the dry bushland reaches to the water's edge. There are tropical forests in both parks as well as extensive patches of thorn.

But most of this region is part of the African savanna and consists of grassland with scattered trees. At times it reminds you of the English countryside except that wild figs, acacia trees and palms take the place of the familiar oaks and elms. There are small lakes and pools in the savanna. Streams with forest-clad banks run down to the great lakes and the Nile.

The main purpose for which National Parks were created in Africa was preservation of the great game animals. These are as much part of the background to the bird life as the countryside itself. There are elephants, hippopotamuses, antelopes, monkeys and many others, but I have written about them in *Wild Animals in an African National Park*. In every type of country there are large numbers of smaller animals such as hares, squirrels, rats and mice which are habitually preyed upon by hawks and eagles. There are great colonies of bats and vast numbers of insects. Among Lizards is the huge varanus monitor lizard which may grow to a length of six feet or more. It is extremely partial to a diet of birds' eggs and is able to climb trees in search of them.

The sort of country that a bird inhabits, together with the creatures that live there, is generally known as its *habitat*. So the lake shores, the forests, the swamps and the savanna all constitute separate habitats. Birds live in a particular habitat because they find there the conditions they need for feeding, breeding and nest-building; with resting and sleeping, these are the occupations on which birds spend most of their time. Over millions of years most different kinds of bird have developed in such a way that their body structure and behaviour fit them for life in certain habitats only.

You can see this quite clearly if you look at the feet, legs, bills and some other features of a few of the better known birds which live in the National Parks. Ducks, cormorants and gulls all have webbed feet. This enables them to swim well and helps them when walking on mud. Herons, of which there are many different kinds, also live near water particularly where there are swamps and marshes. They do not swim and their feet are not webbed, but they have long toes which make it easy for them to walk on soft, wet ground. They also have long legs on which they can wade into the water, making long necks a necessity: they must be able to reach down to the ground in order to feed.

Bustards also have long legs, but they live where the grassland is hard and dry under-foot. They tend to run, or walk, more often than they fly so their toes are short and thick, and they have no backward-pointing toe. To run freely and easily, a bustard needs to have only a small amount of foot-surface in contact with the ground, just as we run on our toes if we wish to run fast. By contrast, the feet of perching birds act as efficient gripping devices enabling them to hold tightly to the branches on which they sit. The grip is automatic. When the bird is asleep, the muscles of its feet tighten so that its grip becomes more secure.

All hawks and eagles have powerful talons for seizing and killing their prey. But the shape of their wings varies with the habitat in which they normally live and hunt. Falcons, such as the Peregrine and Lanner Falcons, have long pointed wings. They are birds of the wide open spaces. Sparrowhawks and Goshawks hunt in the woodlands. Their wings are shorter and more rounded.

The shape of a bird's bill is a good general guide to its diet and may give some idea of the sort of country it inhabits. Herons, for example, have sharp, straight bills which serve as daggers to kill fish, frogs and other small animals. Wading birds, such as snipe and sandpipers, have long, pliable bills with which they probe for insects in the sand, mud-flats and marshes on which they live. Fishing birds are equipped with various special devices. Pelicans, for instance, have pouched bills for storing fish. Cormorants have a hook at the tip of their upper mandibles and this is useful both for catching and holding fish – the upper and lower parts of the bill are known as mandibles. Other birds again have a saw-edge

Black-headed Herons in mutual display at their nest

A Hammerhead standing on top of its nest

A Fish Eagle feeds on an Elephant's trunk

to their bills, the best of all developments for gripping slippery prey.

Hawks and eagles have strong hooked bills for tearing flesh. Parrots also have hooked bills, but these are formed in such a way that the upper and lower mandibles can be moved separately. This enables the parrot to use its bill like a pair of pincers, to crack up the hard seeds and nuts that it eats, and to hold on to branches as it climbs about. Most of the smaller perching birds, in Africa as in Europe, eat either seeds or insects. Seed-eaters, such as finches, tend to have short, stout bills with which they crush and nibble hard seeds. The bills of insect-eating birds are longer, softer and more pointed.

A bird's bill is not used only for feeding. In several respects it functions rather like a human hand. It is used for preening and cleaning the feathers, and for applying oil taken from the oil, or preen, gland which is present at the base of the tail of most kinds of bird. It also serves as a weapon against enemies and as a tool for nest-building. Material is gathered, carried to the nest-site and placed in position almost entirely with the bill. Later, when there are young birds which have to be fed, nearly all their food is carried to the nest in their parents' bills.

The nest is not a home in which the bird lives throughout the year. It is the place chosen, or built, for laying eggs and bringing up the young family. The type of nest depends largely upon the habitat, if only because this determines the material available.

Birds' resting and sleeping places are described as roosts and are sometimes, but certainly not always, near their nests. Most birds sleep soundly with their heads along their backs and their bills tucked into their shoulder feathers. However, storks and pigeons, among others, sleep with their bills pointing forward, and many wading birds go to sleep standing on one leg. A secure roost is just as important as a secure nest, for sleeping birds are particularly vulnerable to predators. Different species achieve this security in different ways. Some of the little African finches, for example, sleep together in great flocks, while others change their roosting places regularly. Other birds again fly to the topmost branches of trees, or roost in holes in steep banks or cliffs.

There are many different kinds of birds' nests, though all nests have the same essential purposes: to provide a support for the eggs and young birds; to provide these with protection; and to produce the warmth necessary to allow the parent bird to incubate the eggs. Different kinds of bird achieve these purposes in different ways, those of the same species invariably following the same practice. Most kinds of bird make some sort of nest, however, though a few lay their eggs in nests already made by other species.

Some birds nest on the ground, using a depression in the soil which they may line with grass, moss or feathers. Most wading birds make this kind of nest; so do many of the birds which live in dry, stony, treeless country. Stone Curlews, for example, simply scrape out little hollows in which to lay their eggs. Another type of nest is a hole in the ground or in a tree. Although this is usually bored out by the bird itself, birds occasionally use holes or cavities that they find. Kingfishers excavate neat round holes in steep, sandy cliffs or banks, and you can see those made by the Pied Kingfisher at many places near the shores of the great lakes and the Nile. Woodpeckers bore into the trunks of trees with their needle-sharp bills to look for food as well as to make their nests. Several different kinds of bird, including herons and storks and cormorants, make hollowed-out platforms of sticks which they build in the forks of trees or on convenient rocks.

Most of the European perching birds make cup-shaped nests which are not covered on top. While nests of this kind are also found in Africa, a majority of the smaller African birds cover their nests with some sort of lid. Others make nests like purses, or small round baskets, with an entrance hole at the side. Some nests of this type, notably those made by the Weaver Birds, are actually woven. Such nests give much better protection against enemies than open cup-shaped nests.

Birds in Africa, where there are countless predatory animals, live surrounded by enemies. Mongooses, wild cats and the larger lizards welcome a meal of eggs or young birds, and most are skilful climbers. There are large numbers of hawks and other birds of prey. There are also many different kinds of snake, some of which eat eggs whenever they get the opportunity.

The green tree-snake, or boomslang, which is widespread in wooded country in both National Parks, is a persistent egg-eater. The small, thin egg-eating snake, *Dasypeltis*, eats hardly anything except eggs. This snake is almost toothless and can swallow an egg the size of a hen's egg. As the egg goes down the snake's gullet, it is stopped by small bones which project into its throat. Moving these bones by means of muscular contractions of its body the snake saws through the egg-shell. It spits out the shell and swallows the contents.

Covering their nests is not the only way in which birds protect themselves against predators. Some nests are suspended over water. Others are built in inaccessible places such as high cliffs or vertical banks. Others again are built close to colonies of bees or other aggressive insects. Some of the many different kinds of warbler, little birds which usually live in woodlands or thickets, often adopt this strategy; so do some other birds. I was once savagely attacked by bees when approaching the nest of a heron which had built on a rock where the bees were swarming. Again, small birds sometimes build close to the nests of such large birds as storks and occasionally eagles. They may do this for protection, as the big bird leaves its little neighbour alone and may get some advantage from the presence of a bird more wary than itself.

When they do not adopt any other protective device, birds use various means to make their nests inconspicuous; an obvious example is that they nearly always use the grass, leaves or twigs of the place in which they are nesting. Birds which make no true nest at all often take advantage of natural camouflage. For instance, Plovers' and Stone Curlews' eggs look so much like stones that they are almost indistinguishable from their surroundings, while the birds themselves are the same colour as the ground on which they sit.

Some other birds protect themselves in an entirely different way. They do not disguise their nests but collect together in large numbers, usually with others of their own kind but sometimes with birds of different species. This is called 'colonial nesting' and is based partly on the well known principle of safety in numbers. It is also believed that, with certain species, the presence of a large number of birds may actually encourage breeding in some way. Pelicans, herons and bee-eaters are among those which normally nest in colonies.

Whatever kind of nest is made, all birds of the same species always build the same sort of nest without having to be shown or taught what to do. This is because nest-building is instinctive, part of the bird's 'breeding behaviour'. All kinds of bird do not behave in the same way at this time; but, when the breeding season arrives, changes take place in certain glands inside the birds' bodies. This starts a sequence of events which follows a very similar pattern, at least with most song-birds. Firstly, some of the male bird's feathers change colour so that he adopts what is known as his 'breeding plumage'. He then chooses a breeding ground, or territory, and occupies this. He sings lustily at this stage to warn off rival males as well as to attract a mate. If another male of his own species intrudes, it will be threatened, chased and possibly attacked.

Eventually the male's song is answered, and a female bird arrives. The male struts about and displays his feathers to her. This is his 'courtship display' and takes very different forms with different species. At this time he usually sings a special 'breeding song', sometimes known as his 'display call', and his mate may answer with different notes. He may bring her 'courtship gifts' of food or nesting materials. Then the two birds will mate.

Nest-building may take place before or after mating. There are also great differences in the length of time actually spent building the nest which may take only a few days or may take several weeks. Again, with most species, the male and female birds play different roles in the work of building the nest though they may work together. However, in Africa where they are surrounded by so many dangers, birds usually build more slowly and carefully than their European relatives even when making the same kind of nest.

Egg-laying follows nest-building after an interval which varies greatly with the different kinds of bird. The female usually sits alone. In many species, however, this duty is shared by the two birds; sometimes the male even sits alone. When incubation is complete, and the eggs hatch out, the parents feed the young birds with food specially collected for this purpose. This goes on until the nestlings are ready to fly and fend for themselves. Most nests are then abandoned.

In Europe, birds breed in the spring each year, all birds nesting at more or less the same time. This is almost certainly the result of the longer, warmer days and the better opportunities of feeding which come with them. In the tropics, the hours of daylight vary little, and there are no great changes in temperature. But there are wet seasons, and dry seasons when much of the countryside is burnt by grass-fires. Breeding takes place at most times of the year but always when food is plentiful and easy to obtain. This varies with the different kinds of bird. For instance, birds which live on seeds and fruits generally find that these are most easily obtained during the rains. But eagles can see their prey most easily when the grass is short and the trees leafless, so they breed in the dry season. Even so, most birds seem to breed during the rains. On and near the equator, which is the situation of the National Parks, there are two rainy seasons. This means that some birds are likely to be in their breeding plumage, or at their nests, at almost any time of the year.

To complete this background picture one special group of birds must be mentioned briefly. These are the migrants, which move from one country to another seasonally or periodically. A number of the birds on the Uganda National Parks list are winter visitors from Europe – for instance, there are birds, particularly waders, which spend the summer months on northern coasts and winter near the shores of Lake Edward. Others travel from one part of Africa to another. More will be said about bird migration later, but it is worth mentioning at this stage that all the birds are not present all the time. The resident birds usually spend most of the year in the same habitat though not necessarily in the same part of it. These form the majority.

2

Pelicans and other Birds
of the Great Lakes

The Kazinga Channel, a twenty-mile stretch of rather sluggish water, joins Lake George to Lake Edward. It is the heart of the Queen Elizabeth National Park where I lived for five years. Every day I watched the elephants and other animals come down to the channel to bathe and drink surrounded by water birds. Schools of hippopotamuses spend the day in shallow water on both sides of the channel and, indeed, all round the shores of the two great lakes. They leave the water at night to graze on land and occasionally spend a few hours basking on the shore during the daytime. Fish are very plentiful in the waters of the channel, and the bird life is magnificent in its abundance and variety.

You can travel up and down the channel by launch and watch all this wildlife. It is little disturbed by the movement of a boat, and I have counted more than forty different kinds of bird in less than an hour spent on board one of the National Park launches. Birds often congregate on one particular sandbank which is also a favourite basking place for hippos. There are almost always gulls, cormorants, pelicans, storks and geese. Restless, sparrow-sized Little Stints, which are common small waders, move about busily and actively among the larger birds. A low cliff immediately behind this sandbank is punctured by kingfishers' nesting holes.

About half a mile beyond this spot, the channel opens out into Lake Edward. Most of the shore-line between is fringed with fresh green grass where you often see a single heron standing motionless. This is not the familiar Grey Heron, but the Goliath Heron, a much larger and more richly coloured bird, standing well over three feet tall. Several acacia trees, which are favoured for nesting by many kinds of bird, stand a few yards back from the water. Elsewhere the banks of the channel are well covered with evergreen thickets where small birds are always visible. Other birds perch on the strange, cactus-like euphorbia trees with which the thickets are interspersed. There are large patches of papyrus reeds where the bird life is almost completely hidden. Only those who know how to look for small details, such as movements in the reeds, are able to see anything at all.

There are always Pied Kingfishers hovering over the channel. A few Darters, birds with sharp bills and long snake-like necks, swim in deeper water, disappearing occasionally as they dive for fish. Fish Eagles soar overhead. Launches on the channel are invariably followed by flocks of terns, gull-like birds sometimes called 'sea-swallows'. A few birds walk, or perch uncertainly, on the backs of hippopotamuses where these stick up above the surface. A grey-brown Common Sandpiper stands upon a hippo's head.

Pied Kingfishers are by far the commonest of the ten species of kingfishers living in the National Parks. They are slightly larger than the bright blue European Kingfisher, which is the only species found in Europe, and are black and white birds with small crests on their heads. Like all kinds of kingfisher, whether eighteen-inch giants or four-inch pigmies, Pied Kingfishers are compact, thick-set birds with large heads, short necks, short legs, short stumpy tails and strong, sharp bills. They all make sudden movements and fly rapidly with quick beats of their little rounded wings. Pied Kingfishers seldom perch. They hover over the water with their bills and tails pointing downwards and their wings beating furiously. If you watch one for any length of time you will see it hover, then move a few yards, stop in mid-air and hover again. Every few minutes it plunges headlong into the water, though you seldom seem to see one emerging with a fish. These kingfishers are particularly plentiful on the Kazinga Channel, and someone once counted eleven hundred during the course of a single boat journey from Lake Edward to Lake George. There were fifty Pied Kingfishers to each mile of water, and they were all either hovering or plunging.

This habitat is ideal for kingfishers. The supply of fish is unlimited, and the steep banks provide excellent nesting places. The kingfishers burrow into the banks with their bills, and scrape away the loose sand and earth with their feet. The burrows, which are not lined, may be a yard or more in depth. When there are eggs or young, both parents share the duties of incubating and of collecting food. Pied Kingfishers breed at least twice each year and do so at almost any season: they have been observed nesting during eight different months.

Another kind of kingfisher which favours the Kazinga Channel is the Malachite Crested Kingfisher. These are tiny birds, brilliantly coloured, greenish-blue, ultramarine and chestnut with red bills and red feet. They look like jewels as they balance on reeds, or even grass, at the water's edge. Like Pied Kingfishers, they plunge for fish and aquatic insects, but they seldom hover. They have the habit of raising and lowering their crests as they fly and of turning abruptly on their perches. At one moment you are looking at their fronts and the next you find yourself looking at their backs which are quite differently coloured. Most of these lovely little birds breed at some distance from the channel, making their burrows away from water or in the banks of narrower streams. Sometimes they nest underground, and I have heard of one being dug out of the side of an ant-bear's hole.

The Malachite Kingfisher is one of the smallest birds of the region. The Marabou Stork, a hideous black and white bird which stands nearly four feet tall, is the largest. It is also the world's largest stork. Marabous are often seen by the channel but are more plentiful in the neighbourhood of the various fishing villages. You see them standing around the outskirts of these villages, looking dejected and bored as they wait for the chance to feed. They eat carrion of all sorts, and have a special liking for fish-carrion and the refuse left by fishermen.

Marabous have naked heads and necks and huge, heavy, straight bills. They also have an extraordinary pouch of bare pink skin, up to twelve inches long, hanging down below their throats. No one knows the function of this pouch which swings about whenever the bird moves. It is not used for storing food as is generally believed, but may possibly play some part in display. Although the pouch looks repulsive to us, it may well appear attractive to other Marabous. They are ugly awkward-looking birds and are so heavy that they have to run along the ground before they can take off. But Marabous carry some surprisingly beautiful white plumes upon their bellies and, once airborne, seem to change completely. With their enormous wing-span they can stay in the air for hours at a time, soaring and cruising at a great height without apparent effort.

Marabous roost on the topmost branches of the euphorbia trees which grow along the banks of the channel. Their weight soon damages the trees, however, so that they are always having to move on to find new roosts. Marabous nest in colonies, often with pelicans or other birds, and make clumsy great nests where the males and females share the various duties. They continue nesting in the same trees for many years.

The Yellow-billed Stork or Wood Ibis, a much more handsome bird, is also seen beside the channel where it habitually frequents the sandbanks. It is called 'ibis' because its bill curves slightly downwards, an ibis characteristic, though the bird is a true stork in all respects. The Wood Ibis stands just under three feet and is rather like the European White Stork except that its tail is black and there is a slightly pinkish tinge to the feathers of its back. It has a bare red face, a splendid orange bill and pink legs.

Wood Ibises usually feed on fish, or on frogs and insects collected from shallow water in which they stand absolutely still, ready to make a quick jab with their powerful bills. They fly beautifully and often dive towards the ground from a height, the rush of air through their wing-feathers producing a distinctly audible sound. Wood Ibises nest in open swamps and marshes and have a pleasing way of standing on their nests shading their young from the heat of the sun.

As you travel along the Kazinga Channel, the nests you see most often are those of the splendid African Fish Eagle, a bird whose immaculate plumage is worth looking at in detail. Its head, the upper part of its back, its breast and tail are pure white. Its wings are black and its belly and shoulders dark chestnut. It is not quite as large as the Golden Eagle and looks very much like the Bald Eagle of America, national emblem of the United States.

Fish Eagles are found throughout the inland waters of Africa wherever conditions are right and the fishing good. They build rather untidy nests among the topmost branches of trees growing near the water. There is a Fish Eagle's nest every few hundred yards along the banks of the channel and much of the coast-line of the two lakes. You can always see the birds themselves: flying, fishing or perching proudly on a branch and uttering their distinctive, lonely cries with their heads thrown back upon their shoulders.

Fish Eagles' nests are small by comparison with those made by the Hammerhead, or Hammerkop, which you occasionally see in a lower fork of the same tree. Hammerheads are brown birds with rather short legs. They stand about twelve inches high, the male being slightly larger and darker than the female, and get their name from the backward-pointing crest of feathers on their heads; seen in combination with the wide, flat bill, this looks like a carpenter's claw-hammer. These strange birds fly with their necks stretched forward like storks but have feet like those of herons. They build one of the largest and most remarkable nests made by any kind of bird. It is completely enclosed, except for an entrance porch, and may be as much as five feet across. However, it does not contain three separate chambers as is often stated.

Working together, the male and the female Hammerheads first make an untidy bowl-shaped platform of sticks, straw and reeds. They do most of the work in the early mornings and this stage usually takes three or four days. Next they build up the sides all round to a height of about six inches and follow this with the roof which is worked up from the back. The roof is a dome-shaped, basket-like structure, made of sticks which the Hammerheads lace together using their bills.

Until the roof is half finished, the two birds work together. After this, the female stays in the nest while the male fetches and carries the material. In this way, and working almost continuously, it takes them two or three days to close in the roof. When this has been done, the nest looks like an enormous round ball of sticks and reeds with a small hole at the front or side, so placed that it can be reached only with difficulty. This entrance hole is often immediately above water. The Hammerheads then add a sort of spout or funnel to the hole, and this becomes a porch. Finally they line the inside, and the porch, with mud, adding loose material to the top and sides of the nest to make it warmer and more waterproof.

This extraordinary nest takes five or six weeks to build. It is used for several years, for roosting as well as for breeding, and it seems that a pair of Hammerheads generally has two nests which they occupy alternately. They fly straight into the nest by way of the entrance porch which is so narrow that they then have to creep up into the chamber. They also use the porch as an observation post, and you frequently see them peering out. Eggs are laid about two weeks after the mud lining is finished and are incubated for thirty days, the male and female Hammerheads, which are a most devoted couple, sharing this work. The young birds fly about seven weeks after hatching.

The nest is firm enough for a man to stand on, and provides the birds with almost complete protection against most possible enemies as well as perfect insulation against sun and rain. But small birds, such as sparrows, often make use of part of the nest. Barn Owls, Kestrels and possibly other birds have been known to drive away the Hammerheads and take over the nest for themselves. The huge Eagle Owl, which is much too big to get into the porch, sometimes takes possession of one of these nests before the roof has been put on. The top of the finished nest is widely used as a perch.

Hammerheads feed in the early morning, late evening and even at night, when you hear their sharp, shrill calls as they shuffle their feet about in shallow water disturbing the small creatures they hope to catch and eat. Their diet from the water is chiefly small fish, aquatic insects and crabs; and on land, snails and grasshoppers. They often stand on the backs of wallowing hippos using these great animals as perches from which to hunt and fish.

You frequently see little parties of three or four Hammerheads together, usually close to a nest. They jump and dance around, bow to one another, throw their heads right back on to their shoulders and make a sort of grunting, croaking noise. They also behave like this when courting, adding a cackling call to their dancing action. But Hammerheads breed rather irregularly, and this performance is not limited to breeding behaviour. As you watch then, these birds always give the impression of being very busy.

The Kazinga Channel is not the only place in the Queen Elizabeth Park where you can see these various kinds of bird. They congregate at many points along the shores of both great lakes, and I had several favourite observation points when I was living in the Park. The best was Pelican Point, where one of the mountain streams from the Ruwenzori range forms a small estuary as it enters Lake Edward. As you drive across the bushland on your way to this point you nearly always see elephants. Families of warthogs hurry about the grassland with their tails straight up in the air. Antelopes and buffaloes look up from their grazing without fear. The actual approach to the lake is through almost treeless country except for a few euphorbias and palms. A clump of acacia trees overlooks a small marsh beyond which a spit of hard, dry land protrudes into the lake.

In this small area there are several different habitats close together so that you see many different kinds of bird. The animals add to the fascination of the place, particularly as there are always hippos there. You sometimes see them lying on the spit, tightly packed together, making a strange contrast with the colour and beauty of the birds.

I was once standing at Pelican Point watching a pair of Fish Eagles soaring about two hundred feet above the water. They were circling in a leisurely way, as is their habit, when suddenly the two birds came together and clutched talons in mid-air. Holding their wings out stiffly behind them, they went into a spin and dropped to within thirty feet of the water, their talons still clasped together. Then the Eagles pulled out of their spin and resumed their normal soaring flight; throughout that fantastic drop there had been no loss of control. Fish Eagles are superb fliers always. Sometimes they dive headlong to the water, checking just above the surface. Or, if a fish has been sighted, the eagle may plunge right in, to emerge a few seconds later with its prey held firmly in its claws.

Like other birds of prey, Fish Eagles catch and kill with their talons, using their hooked bills to tear up the flesh when the catch has been landed. A Fish Eagle can take off from the water without much difficulty when carrying a fish up to about three pounds in weight. It will then fly away to eat its prey either on the nearest convenient dry land or high up in a tall tree. Of course, the eagle cannot take off if the fish is too heavy; and I once saw one swimming across the Kazinga Channel with its prey, using its wings in a kind of breast stroke.

Fish Eagles do not always catch their own fish. They do not hesitate to attack another eagle if they chance upon one flying away with its prey, and thrilling contests sometimes take place with the birds showing complete mastery of every trick known to high-speed aerial combat. A Fish Eagle will also attack an Osprey and can almost always make it drop its prey. At times they rob other fish-eating birds and seem to delight in chasing herons, particularly the majestic Goliath Heron at which they sometimes dive when in full flight.

Ospreys are smaller and less brilliantly coloured than Fish Eagles, and they are seen only occasionally on Lake Edward. The habits of the two birds are much the same except that the Osprey, whose wings are thinner and more pointed, tends to fly low over the water and plunge in with half-closed wings.

The pelicans, which give Pelican Point its name, are the most striking of the birds that you see there. They are of two kinds: the great White Pelican and the slightly smaller Pink-backed Pelican. Their habits are very similar and, on Lake Edward, you usually see them together. They both feed almost entirely on fish, and have the habit of doing things in groups: nesting, roosting, fishing and flying, for example. They look clumsy on the ground, and seem to find difficulty in taking off, but are magnificent performers in the air. Pelicans frequently fly in V-formation like geese. At other times they spiral and fly to great heights with their necks doubled back and hardly a beat of their huge wings – White Pelicans have a wing-span of about nine feet. You see them gliding down to the water after a long flight looking like so many flying-boats, landing with a bow-wave and a cloud of spray.

One of the pelican's most remarkable features is the pouch attached to its lower jaw. This has a capacity of over three gallons – more than twice that of the bird's stomach. The pouch is used both as a net for catching fish and as a bag in which to hold the catch for a short time. A single fish is swallowed at once. But, if a pelican gets into a shoal, it scoops up as many fish as possible and only stops when its pouch is fully stretched so that it can hold no more. Then the pelican allows the water to drain away, closes its bill and swallows the catch. Occasionally the pouch has to be dried and aired. The bird stands with its head up, its great mouth wide open, and the pouch spread out across its chest.

In spite of their great interest, pelicans always seem to make people smile. This may be because of the well known rhyme of the pelican's 'beak holding more than its belly can' – an old joke but an absolutely true statement as we have seen. Or it may be because of their absurdly pompous appearance as they waddle about on land. The pelican's habit of resting with its great bill against its chest was probably the origin of the ancient belief that it fed its young with blood drawn from its own breast. Of course, this is not true. To mediaeval minds, however, this myth identified pelicans with Christ's suffering on the cross, and it is often depicted on carved bench-ends and other decorations in old churches.

Pelican Point is ideal for the pelicans' habit of fishing in troops, and you may see them doing this in several different ways. They usually advance in line, sometimes swimming slowly forward, and all dipping their heads together as if answering a signal. At other times they beat the water with their wings and feet to drive the

Egyptian Geese

Yellow-billed Stork or
Wood Ibis at nest

Skimmers about to land on a sand-bank; a Crocodile in the water nearby
is almost covered by water-lilies

Shoe-bill or Whale-headed Stork   Sacred Ibis carrying nesting material

fish towards the shallows. Then they all plunge their great bills into the water and scoop the fish into their pouches. Occasionally the pelicans gather into a half circle to surround a shoal of fish, raising their wings as they plunge their heads into the water. Neither the White Pelican nor the Pink-backed Pelican is able to dive. They are most effective fishers, nevertheless, for each bird catches and eats about four pounds of fish each day.

Pelicans nest in large colonies, and to do this they often travel several miles from the waters where they fish. There are hundreds of pelicans living in the Queen Elizabeth Park, for instance, but there are no known nesting places there; the nearest nests are in the Congo a few miles away from the southern end of Lake Edward. The Pink-backed Pelicans nest there, sharing a riverside forest of palm and euphorbia trees with a colony of Marabou Storks. Both kinds of pelican usually make their nests on the crowns of quite tall trees. Storks do the same. In other parts of Africa, however, the White Pelicans sometimes nest on the ground in a most haphazard way.

Young pelicans are not able to fly for about two months after hatching out of the eggs. Throughout that time they have to be fed by their parents, both of whom help in this work. They take it in turns to fly to the water and catch as much fish as they can. They swallow this, half digest it in their stomachs, and then bring it up again into their pouches from which the young birds feed as if from a bowl. Although pelicans have hardly any voice, the clapping of bills and the flapping of wings produces a great deal of noise at these nesting places.

Pelicans grow up slowly, taking about three years to reach maturity. They live for a very long time and, like a few other large species, have been known to survive for over fifty years in captivity. But birds generally live longer in zoos than in the wilds where they have to face so many dangers, and where many die or are killed while still young. Even so, there are numerous

3

records of wild birds living to a good age. A gull has been known to live for over thirty years, a heron for twenty-four years, a cormorant for eighteen years, a swallow for fifteen years and a sparrow for ten. Generally speaking, the larger the bird, the longer it is likely to live.

Cormorants and Darters are, after pelicans, the most important fish-eating birds living on the great lakes. There are two kinds of cormorant: the Common Cormorant and the smaller Long-tailed Cormorant. The Common Cormorant of East Africa is the same species as the familiar bird of Britain's coasts. It is a large blue-black bird with some bronze and dark grey in its plumage. The British Cormorant has a small patch of white on its throat and thighs. The African Cormorant has a white front to its neck and a white breast, so that it is sometimes called the White-necked Cormorant; the male develops a round white patch on his side when in his breeding plumage. The Long-tailed Cormorant is wholly black and silver-grey except that the male grows a few white feathers behind his eyes during the breeding season.

In Britain, cormorants live on the sea coast only visiting inland waters occasionally. In Africa, Common Cormorants are found only on lakes and rivers well away from the sea. Long-tailed Cormorants live by the sea as well as on the fresh water lakes. Both kinds of cormorant are plentiful in Africa.

All cormorants catch their fish by diving under water from the surface, sometimes gaining impetus by means of a little jump. One has been known to stay under water for seventy seconds and reach a depth of fifty feet; but they normally emerge after about half a minute, or sooner if a fish has been caught. They glide about under the water with their wings held slightly away from their bodies, and they catch a fish by suddenly extending their necks and nipping it with the formidable hook on their bills. Immediately a cormorant has made a successful catch it swims to the surface. It then swallows the fish head first, juggling it around, throwing it into the air and catching it again if it happens to be the wrong way round – most fish-eating birds find it necessary to swallow fish head first. A cormorant eats a little more than one pound of fish daily, occasionally taking a crab or a frog as well.

Cormorants do not stay in the water longer than is necessary, and rarely rest on the surface when not actually fishing. They retire to the land when they have had enough to eat and rest on the ground, on a rock or on the branch of a tree. The Long-tailed Cormorant seems to prefer a branch, which is probably more convenient for its tail.

You often see cormorants on land, standing on their feet with their heads quite still and their wings half open as if they are being dried in the sun. No one is absolutely certain why they do this. It may be that their wings, which are much larger than the wings of most other diving birds, really have to be dried in this way. Or it may be that cormorants find this position comfortable and that it helps them to digest their food. Most fishing birds are able to stay in the water almost indefinitely, and 're-proof' their plumage by smearing their feathers with oil taken from their oil glands. It is certainly possible that cormorants' feathers are less efficiently waterproofed than those of most other water-birds although they do not feel as if they lacked oil. Cormorants sometimes get caught up in fishing nets on Lake Edward, and I have rescued several from this predicament, invariably getting myself into an oily mess while doing so.

Cormorants give the impression of feeling the heat more seriously than most birds. By the Kazinga Channel, particularly, you often see them standing around panting violently with their bills half-open and their throats working rapidly. Birds cannot sweat, so that panting is an important way of keeping cool.

When a male cormorant is ready to breed, he goes to the place of his choice, raises his tail, draws in his head and neck, and flaps his wings. If another male approaches, he raises his tail straight up, throws his head back several times, shakes his half-open bill in a threatening way and makes a loud croaking noise. In fact, he gives a very good exhibition of 'threat display'. When the female arrives, however, he opens his bill as wide as he can in an action that looks like yawning. She responds with the same action and a perky cocking up of her tail. With courting successfully under way, the two birds build their nest together. They sometimes nest in trees, and sometimes on rocks, always using sticks and debris collected from the shore. Cormorants nest, as they roost, in colonies with others of their own kind.

Young cormorants develop slowly. They can swim and dive at about five weeks but cannot fly until they are at least two months old. Their flying action is very much like that of geese. Before they can fly, however, young Long-tailed Cormorants are able to clamber about their nesting trees, using their bills like hands to hold on to branches. When the chicks are very young, they are fed on half-digested fish which is dripped into their mouths off the hook of the parent bird's bill. At a slightly later stage the parent bird holds the food in its own gullet. The chick plunges its head right down its parent's throat, which can be stretched considerably to make this strange action possible. The elasticity of its throat also enables a cormorant to swallow quite large fish. Many young cormorants are lost during their first year, as the chicks are often stolen from their nests by other birds. One of their most dangerous neighbours is the Grey-headed Gull.

There are quite large numbers of Darters on these lakes. You sometimes see them on their own, but they often join the cormorants to which they are closely related. They are about the same size as the Common Cormorant but are thinner and less sturdy. They have longer necks, long sharp-pointed bills and long stiff tails. Darters share many of the cormorant's habits and fish in much the same way except that they usually stab their prey in preference to catching it in their bills. When hunting under water,

Darters keep their necks folded back on to their shoulders, almost in the shape of the letter 'S', and then shoot their heads forward when within striking range of their prey.

Darters are often called Snake Birds because of the shape of their necks and their habit of swimming with their bodies submerged and only their heads and necks showing above the surface. Like cormorants, they stand as though drying their wings after a spell of fishing, and only enter the water to escape danger or to feed. They take off clumsily from the surface but fly well, with their tail feathers spread out and a slight kink in their long necks. For roosting and nesting, they favour the wooded borders of lakes and streams, often building so that their nests overhang the water. I have frequently seen a Darter sitting calmly on the head of a hippopotamus with its wings spread out.

You see several different kinds of gull on the great lakes but the commonest, by far, is the Grey-headed Gull. It is a white bird with a grey head and some black on its wings; its bill, legs and feet are red; in general appearance it resembles the Black-headed Gull which is so familiar in parts of Britain. Like most gulls, Grey-headed Gulls eat almost anything they can find, including fish and small water-animals. They also eat eggs and take young birds from their nests, flying away with them held firmly in their bills. Grey-headed Gulls often make their own nests near nesting colonies of other birds, such as cormorants, so that they can prey upon them. These gulls also catch insects when in flight and, in this, they behave rather like terns. Sometimes also they pick up molluscs and drop them from a height. It is uncertain if this is a form of play, or if they are trying to break the shells so as to get at the contents.

White-winged Black Terns follow boats on the Kazinga Channel, so that they can feed on small fish which are killed and cut up by the propellers. They are active, restless fliers, sometimes rising and hovering in the air, sometimes skimming the surface or diving right into the water to harpoon little fish on their exceedingly sharp bills.

The real homeland of these terns is in eastern Europe and central Asia. Large numbers visit East Africa during the winter, however, and many now live permanently on the great lakes where conditions are excellent for them. Usually you see them in their non-breeding dress, when they are white birds with their upper parts blotched and speckled black, and with red legs and black bills that show a little red at the base. In breeding plumage, they are sharply black and white except for the upper side of the wing which is grey. Their bills are then dark red. In the Queen Elizabeth Park they are seldom seen in this plumage, and breeding has not yet been observed. In Hungary, where they are extremely numerous during the summer, they breed in open marshes and flooded meadows. They make their nests of marsh grasses and decaying vegetation, sometimes placing these on floating platforms of water lilies.

Gull-billed Terns are also fairly common during the European winter. They are larger than White-winged Black Terns, fourteen inches long compared with nine inches, and you see them sitting on the water like gulls. They seldom dive.

Ducks and geese do not like swimming on the great lakes, probably because of the large predatory lung-fish which is as ready to feed upon birds as upon other fish. A lung-fish may weigh as much as a hundred pounds and is one of the few kinds of fish that actually breathes air. But you see large numbers of Egyptian Geese at many places along the lake shores and the channel banks. They seem to enjoy the company of elephants and hippopotamuses, and I have often watched them strutting about unconcernedly among the feet of these great animals. Egyptian Geese do not spend very much time actually in the water as they feed largely on grass and other land vegetation. But they take their young goslings for a swim soon after they are hatched. It is charming to see the little flotillas swimming about among the hippos whose presence probably keeps the lung-fish away.

Egyptian Geese are rather like European Shelduck. They are brownish-coloured birds, with some black and white in their plumage and a broad glossy green band behind their shoulders; their eyes are surrounded by a large chestnut-coloured ring. They nest in a greater variety of places than most birds. In the Queen Elizabeth Park, these geese usually choose ground near water where there are shrubs to provide them with shelter. They use grass and reeds to build their nests, which they line with a fine grey down. In some places, however, they use holes dug out in the ground or make their nests in trees; and they have been known to settle into a half-made Hammerhead's nest. Egyptian Geese make a quacking honk and hiss loudly when angry.

Huge swamps fringe the shores of Lake George and block up sheltered bays and backwaters beside Lake Edward and the Kazinga Channel. They consist almost entirely of papyrus reeds which grow ten feet tall from a base of rotting stems. The result is a dense mat of vegetation, great chunks of which break off from time to time to become floating islands.

It is not easy to see birds in the papyrus, though this does not mean that they are not there. There are little Swamp Warblers and Reed Warblers, small brownish birds which feed largely on insects and have loud musical calls. There are also two interesting kinds of shrike, predatory birds about the size of a thrush, whose habits will be described in a later chapter. These are the Red-breasted Shrike, or Gonolek, and the Black-headed Gonolek respectively. Both are black birds with crimson breasts; one has a yellow head, the other a black head. You have to look very carefully, and have a good deal of luck, to see either of these shrikes, but they will sometimes emerge from the swamps for a short time if they hear a strange noise. They themselves have interesting, though not very beautiful, calls. The male and female

Black-headed Gonolek appear to sing duets. The male gives a whistling 'yoicking' call. The female answers with a cry that has been compared to the sound of tearing cloth.

Some members of the heron family, such as Bitterns and Night Herons, also live in these swamps. They are quite unlike typical herons which are tall, stately birds with graceful movements. Bitterns and Night Herons are short-legged, short-necked, rather squat and given to furtive movements. The European Bittern visits Africa but has not yet been seen in the National Parks. However, the African Little Bittern, which looks very much like the European Little Bittern, lives there. It is a brownish-coloured bird and only stands about ten inches high with its neck fully stretched. It is solitary and secretive in its habits. The Night Heron, about twice the size of a Little Bittern, is equally secretive and rarely moves except at night. It is coloured dark green and white which makes it particularly difficult to see among the papyrus reeds.

All kinds of bittern depend upon camouflage when in danger. Instead of running or flying away, they stay absolutely still with their bills pointing straight upwards in a way that makes them look remarkably like the reeds among which they live.

The Little Bitterns nest in these reeds, and feed on insects and marsh-life generally. They search for their food in the mud and, in doing so, get their feathers all covered with slime. So they have developed an elaborate toilet routine. The bittern first rubs its head and neck on the patches of soft downy feathers which all herons have on their breasts. These feathers give off a fine dust which the bird uses for cleaning its bill. Then it combs itself with the saw-like under-surface of its middle toe, and this removes most of the mud and mess. After this the bittern preens carefully, passing its feathers through its bill. Then, still using its bill, it anoints itself all over with oil from its oil gland. The bird is soon ready to get into a mess all over again.

Night Herons live in many European Countries but only appear in Britain occasionally. They occur also in Asia and in parts of eastern and southern Africa, but they are not really common anywhere. The swamps which border the great lakes make an ideal habitat for them, however.

Their courtship dancing is perhaps the most interesting thing about Night Herons. The male, whose legs became rosy red in the breeding season, performs a strange little dance on the place he has chosen for his nest. He moves from one foot to the other, hunches his shoulders and lowers his head and wings. Then he utters his deep, low courting cry. If a female appears in answer to this, he brings his head down to ground level, twists it to one side and makes his greeting call. Afterwards he raises his head, and fluffs up the feathers on the crown of his head, his neck and his back. He stands with his eyes protruding from their sockets, exposing the red iris, and bows to his mate with his plumes falling over his head. Then he utters his greeting call again. It is difficult to believe, after all this, that any female Night Heron could refuse to join him at his nest.

3

Birds and Beasts of the River Nile

The Nile runs through the Murchison Falls National Park, cutting the area more or less in half. For sixty miles the river is a broad, rushing torrent. Then it forces its way through a narrow gap in the rock and plunges down one hundred and thirty feet over the Murchison Falls themselves. Emerging from this rocky gorge, the river opens out and becomes a smooth, but still fast-flowing, sheet of water. Fifteen miles further on the Nile enters Lake Albert. From the lake it turns north to become, for about twenty miles, the western boundary of the Park.

Above the Falls, you can visit the river at a few points only. On the quieter waters below, you can travel by launch for several miles and watch the birds and animals beside the river: one of the most fascinating experiences that Africa has to offer. There are thousands upon thousands of colourful water-lilies on the open river. Nile cabbages (*Pistia stratiotes*) float on the surface of the more sheltered backwaters which they cover almost completely.

All this floating vegetation provides perfect conditions for the Jacanas, or Lily-trotters, which are familiar birds on many of the rivers, lakes and pools throughout a large part of Africa. They look rather clumsy, standing about ten inches high with long legs and immensely long toes. But their plumage is beautiful: they are chestnut-brown and have a golden collar and a bald, blue patch on the forehead. The female is slightly larger than the male, though in all other respects they are the same. You usually see a pair of Lily-trotters together, and there may be two or three pairs in the same locality as these birds seldom move far unless forced to do so by flooding.

Lily-trotters swim well and dive well but are not good fliers, seeming to find their long legs and feet awkward to manage when they are in the air. On short flights their legs simply hang straight down. On longer flights they trail their legs out behind their bodies, bringing them forward as they approach the ground; they also raise their wings vertically above their backs as they come in to land.

Lily-trotters are fascinating to watch as they walk delicately across the floating vegetation seldom hurrying unless hunting for insects, such as the water-beetles which form the greater part of their diet. They can balance on the most flimsy leaves, thanks to the development of their feet and the wide spread of their toes which effectively distributes the load. Lily-trotters judge perfectly whether or not a leaf is firm enough to bear their weight. They skip gracefully from one floating leaf to another, helped by a flick of their pointed wings. I have a delightful memory of this. A Lily-trotter, accompanied by one small chick, was moving slowly across a bed of Nile cabbages. Immediately behind them, there was a mother hippopotamus with a very young calf. The hippo apparently objected to my boat and came barging through the leaves with the intention of driving us off. The Lily-trotters skipped neatly out of the way, but only just in time.

These strange birds do not make proper nests. They simply lay their eggs on bunches of overlapping water-lilies or Nile cabbages, or on little piles of rotting vegetation at the edge of the water. The eggs are beautifully marked and look as if they have been polished. Their shells are much thicker than those of most eggs, probably to give them adequate protection against water. Young Lily-trotters are active almost immediately they are hatched. They

can swim and dive at once and sometimes hide from danger under-
neath floating leaves. A Lily-trotter has been seen carrying its
young chick, tucked against its breast and under its bill.

Pratincoles often hawk for insects above the cauldron of tur-
bulent water immediately below the Falls. They are starling-
sized birds with short legs, pointed wings and plumage which is
mainly a dull brown relieved by some black and white. They have
forked tails like terns, fly rather like swallows, and are particularly active in the evenings when they zig-zag backwards and
forwards, twittering and screaming as they catch insects on the
wing.

You see little flocks of pratincoles sitting on a rock or on open
ground near water. They sit hunched up and keep very still, all
facing into the wind. They would be difficult to see but for their
habit of craning their short necks and raising their heads when
they suspect that anyone is observing them. As they fly down on to
a rock, pratincoles raise their wings up above their backs in much
the same way as Lily-trotters. There are several different kinds
of pratincole, but it is extremely difficult to tell them apart. The
White-collared Pratincole lives on the Nile; two other species
visit the area at certain seasons.

A short distance down the river, you often see a flock of
Skimmers, unusual birds sometimes called Scissor-billed Terns.
They are not there throughout the year as they move away to
other parts of Africa at certain seasons. They are more plentiful
further north, in the Sudan, and appear only rarely in the Queen
Elizabeth Park to the south. Skimmers are about fifteen inches in
length and have long pointed wings and very short legs. They are
brownish-grey in colour, with some black and white in their
plumage, and have large orange-red bills which are very remarkable. The lower mandible is much longer than the upper, and the
two parts fit together in such a way that slippery prey can be held
firmly. This bill is also flattened vertically making it look like the

two blades of a pair of scissors. No other kind of bird has this particular sort of bill.

By the Nile, the Skimmers spend most of the day resting on a sandbank where they sit in a tightly packed little flock. They all take off at the same moment, fly round in a small circle and return to the same sandbank. They fly bunched together with their bills pointing towards the water. They fish at night or late in the evening when you hear their sharp, shrill, whistling calls. Then the Skimmers fly just above the surface of the river, with their lower mandibles actually in the water and using a high wing-stroke which saves their wings from getting wet. They perceive their prey by touch, not by sight as most birds do, and catch whatever knocks against their bills. They flip small fish out of the water and swallow them, without a pause, while still flying.

Skimmers sometimes adopt a very cunning strategy. They fly across the surface of the river, ploughing the water in their usual way. This disturbs a number of minute aquatic insects which, in turn, attract small fish. As soon as the Skimmers have passed, the fish rise to the surface. The birds then turn abruptly in their tracks. They fly back over the same stretch of water with their bills opening and closing rapidly as they collect the spoil.

The headquarters of the Murchison Falls National Park, which includes the Paraa Safari Lodge, one of the places where visitors stay, is situated on the north bank of the Nile about seven miles below the Falls. We kept several boats and launches at Paraa. Some were for the use of visitors. Others were needed by the Wardens for a number of different tasks such as searching for poachers, studying the movement of the elephants, and watching the banks of the river for the presence of any particularly interesting animals or unusual birds. I have often travelled up and down this stretch of the river between Lake Albert and the Murchison Falls, and every journey has been different. I find the Nile even more fascinating than the Kazinga Channel, magnificent as that is, and I am sure that one of the reasons for this is the excitement of fast flowing water. Again, the scenery is much more varied than beside the channel. As you travel along the river the banks are changing continuously.

There are several large papyrus swamps, particularly where the Nile opens out before entering Lake Albert. There are also huge grassy meadows alongside the river. In places the banks are covered in forest. Great mahogany trees with reddish foliage, wild black plums (*Vitex*), sweet-scented crotons with yellow flowers and many other fine forest trees stand close to the water's edge, providing a home for monkeys as well as birds. Where the ground is more open you see the trees of the African savanna: acacias, fig trees and the extraordinary *Kigelia* 'sausage tree' with its great woody fruits. There are also thorny bushes and shrubs of many different kinds. Immediately beside the river, or actually growing out of the water, there are ambatch trees whose wood is lighter than cork and makes excellent floats for fishing nets. There are also sandbanks and a few patches of deep shade provided by dark green *Trichilia* trees.

Animals of several kinds come down to graze in the river-side meadows and drink from the waters of the Nile. You can always see elephants, some of them carrying magnificent tusks. There are usually buffaloes and antelopes as well. Great schools of hippopotamuses spend their days in the river. Giraffes and rhinoceroses come to the northern bank, and you can usually see ox-peckers (pale brown, starling-sized birds) riding on their backs. Dog-faced baboons regularly forage for food at several places on both banks; they are a menace to ground-nesting birds as they eat eggs whenever they can.

Troops of black and white colobus monkeys move like acrobats through the forest trees. With their flowing white manes and well kept coats, they are often mistaken for birds by visitors who are not accustomed to the scene. The flash of white, which first catches your eye, can certainly suggest a Fish Eagle. Fish Eagles are as numerous beside the Nile as they are beside the Kazinga Channel. Indeed you see many of the same kinds of bird on the two stretches of water, though pelicans and cormorants are less common on the Nile.

There are hundreds of crocodiles by the Nile. These great reptiles like to spend most of the day ashore, either sleeping in the shade of the *Trichilia* trees or basking in the open on sunny sandbanks. They nearly always stay close to the water so that they can plunge in immediately if threatened or alarmed. They feed almost entirely in the water, chiefly at night or late in the evening, when they catch the fish that make up most of their diet. At such times they can be very dangerous to human beings, or to other animals, should these wander into the water; but crocodiles seldom attack on land.

You see crocodiles on the sandbanks with their great yellow mouths wide open. Sometimes hippos share the sandbanks with them, and there are nearly always several different kinds of bird about. On land, crocodiles show no interest in the birds, even those such as ducks and geese which are regularly eaten if encountered in the water. The birds, for their part, seem to show no fear of the crocodiles.

Many people are surprised that predators and their prey should be able to remain close together in this way. But creatures which prey upon other animals do not hunt and kill all the time. They do so only if they are hungry, and other creatures seem to know when they are dangerous. For instance, antelopes will continue to graze placidly in the presence of lions which are not actually hunting. Like most other animals, crocodiles have a regular routine. They feed at certain times, rest and sleep at others. Birds most probably know that they are safe when the crocodiles are on land during the day. In any case they are in little danger while there is a plentiful supply of fish in the Nile, and the crocodiles can satisfy their appetites in the way they are accustomed to.

The whole relationship between birds and crocodiles has always been found interesting. Over two thousand years ago, the Greek historian Herodotus wrote that a bird, which he called the *Trochilus*, would enter the open mouths of basking crocodiles to pick their teeth and remove the leeches from their gums and throats. The Roman author, Pliny the Elder, repeated this story and said that the bird was never harmed because the action was of benefit to the crocodile. This ancient story is still told although there is no proof that any bird actually behaves in this way.

Herodotus's 'Crocodile Bird', or *Trochilus*, was probably the Egyptian Plover, a beautiful little bird which looks rather like a pratincole. But it might have been the Spur-winged Plover, a bird which is rather like our Lapwing, about which a similar but even more remarkable story is sometimes told: if the crocodile should close its mouth by mistake, while the bird is still inside, the plover gives a sharp jab with the spur on its wing and the crocodile obediently opens its jaws.

Egyptian Plovers are very tame birds which habitually frequent sandbanks but which are seldom seen along this stretch of the Nile. Spur-winged Plovers are among the commonest birds in the Murchison Falls National Park. I have often seen them standing, walking, feeding and even sleeping close to basking crocodiles. But I have never seen a plover inside a crocodile's mouth, and I have never heard of a reputable naturalist who claims to have done so. It is always a pity to spoil a good story, but this one probably is not true although it is certainly not outside the bounds of possibility.

When 'Crocodile Birds' and plovers are feeding near sleeping crocodiles they occasionally walk up on to their backs as they search for insects. Common Sandpipers, migrants from Europe which you often see on the Nile between October and March,

African Spoonbills at their nests

Lily-trotter or Jacana, showing
elongated feet

Marabou Storks with Stilts, Waders and Lesser Flamingoes

Sacred Ibis on nesting tree

work over crocodiles' scales in the same search. Wagtails sometimes behave in the same way. Crocodiles lie very still when they
are on land and can easily be mistaken for logs of wood. It is even
possible that these various birds simply do not realize that they
are living animals.

The closest association of all is between crocodiles and Water
Thicknees. Water Thicknees belong to a family of birds which
are known as thicknees, stone curlews or dikkops. They are like
plovers but have unusually large, knobbly leg-joints, from which
the name 'thicknee' derives, although the visible joint on the leg
of any kind of bird is the equivalent of an ankle rather than a knee.
They also have great yellow eyes which enable them to see well
in the dark. They eat insects, such as beetles and grasshoppers,
and are usually more active at dusk, or when the moon is shining,
than during the day. Their eerie, wailing cries are frequently
heard at night. Some members of this group of birds live in dry,
open country. Others, including Water Thicknees, frequent
sandy ground near the borders of lakes and rivers.

Water Thicknees do not make proper nests. They sometimes
lay their eggs on dry elephant or hippopotamus droppings but
normally do so on sand, sometimes scraping out little hollows
which they decorate with a few stones, sticks or blades of grass.
The main breeding season of the Water Thicknees is the same as
that of the crocodiles, which also lay their eggs on sand. Crocodiles
bury their eggs, forty or fifty together, beside the water and
cover them over completely. The female crocodile does not incubate her eggs in the way that a bird does. She simply lies close
to where they are buried in order to guard them from the various
animals, such as baboons and monitor lizards, which dig them up
and eat them whenever possible. Water Thicknees frequently
make their nests in the middle of crocodile breeding grounds,
and you often see these quite small birds sitting close to the huge
reptiles.

4

In this strange partnership, the bird and the crocodile help each other. The Water Thicknee is alert and wary while the crocodile is basking in the sun. When an enemy approaches, the bird usually squats down motionless in the hope of avoiding detection. If this ruse fails, however, it gives its noisy, whistling alarm call (which rouses the crocodile) and then darts away with its neck stretched out forward. Thicknees fly weakly and slowly, by means of a series of rapid wing-beats followed by a pause, so they prefer to run along the ground. The crocodile never harms the bird, nor does it damage the eggs when it moves into or out of the water. The Water Thicknees, in their turn, probably find that the presence of a crocodile discourages predators from interfering with the eggs in their rather inadequate nests. When the young hatch out, they are able to move about immediately, another safeguard provided by nature.

Crocodiles have enemies among birds as well as friends. When the young crocodiles are ready to emerge from their eggs, the female scrapes away the sand; the babies then cut their own way out of the shells and make for the water immediately. All the crocodiles of the region hatch out at about the same time, and when this is happening Marabou Storks congregate. They settle near the crocodile beaches and wait for the baby crocodiles to appear. As these scuttle towards the river, the Marabous stab at them with their great bills. Many young crocodiles only live for a few moments, ending their brief lives as a tasty morsel for a Marabou. On the whole, it seems that crocodiles have more to fear from birds than the other way round.

You see Goliath Herons by the Nile even more often than by the Kazinga Channel. They are superb birds, giants among the herons, and they are certainly worthy of their naming after the gigantic Philistine, slain by King David of Judah and Israel. You usually see a single Goliath Heron, standing alone in shallow water, waiting to stab a passing fish with its sharp and powerful bill. Goliaths are generally silent but sometimes utter a deep, raucous call that sounds something like the baying of a hound. They fly with a slow, regular beat of their great wings and seem to find some difficulty in getting themselves into the air. I have often watched them take off and fly away with their wings only just clearing the water.

You occasionally also see Purple Herons. They are not unlike Goliaths but are very much smaller and, of course, are well known in southern Europe. They are not very plentiful and have a tendency to skulk in reed-beds. Nevertheless, a friend of mine once watched a delightful scene involving two of these birds. The male bird flew down on to a beach and began to call in an unmusical, croaking voice. Then the female arrived, and the two birds stood motionless quite close together. The male soon began to dance and show off. After a while, however, he gave up these antics. He dipped his bill into the water, picked up a small stick and offered it to the female. But instead of taking it, she repeated his action, offering him a stick in return. Something unfortunately disturbed the two herons at this stage. They flew away together so that the end of the story was lost. Even so, this was an excellent example of birds exchanging courtship gifts suggestive of nest-building. Herons usually nibble at each other's bills during courtship. Sometimes the male takes the female's bill in his.

These are not the only herons living by the Nile, and I cannot remember ever having done the boat trip to the bottom of the Falls without seeing at least one Great White Heron, or Great White Egret as they are also called. They are no larger than Purple Herons but, owing to their shining white plumage, are even more conspicuous than Goliaths. The smaller egrets are there too, in greater numbers, their white colouring standing out against the green background of the river banks. Their lovely white plumage makes it impossible to mistake an egret for any other kind of bird.

Herons usually nest in colonies, known as heronries, many of which have been occupied for dozens, if not hundreds, of years. Most heronries are used by one kind of heron only, but herons sometimes nest in mixed colonies with birds of other kinds. This may happen simply because more than one species favours the same type of site. Goliath Herons, however, usually nest alone. Occasionally they join mixed colonies, and then they hide their own enormous nests in the middle of the group. This arrangement gives extra protection to the Goliaths whose young are rather prone to falling out of their nests. Nestling Goliaths are not often attacked from above by predatory birds, as they look just like balls of fluff that are not worth eating.

You can see one of these mixed colonies on a certain small, swampy island in the middle of the Nile. Several Goliath Herons nest there every year, on low-growing acacia thorns and ambatch trees. They share the island with a number of Sacred Ibises and with one African Spoonbill, which constantly jabs at the other birds if it finds that they are getting too close. Spoonbills frequently join these mixed colonies, and there is an acacia wood in Kenya, not far from Lake Victoria, where thousands of herons, egrets, ibises and spoonbills nest together. Each year the spoonbills return to the same trees, which are always left vacant for them by the other birds, even though the spoonbills breed two or three weeks later than the herons and the ibises.

These African Spoonbills are very similar to the European Spoonbills. They both resemble small white storks but have long, spoon-shaped bills which spread out at the tip and are used for gathering food, chiefly small shellfish and aquatic insects, in shallow water. The spoonbills wade around, sweeping their bills backwards and forwards with an action that suggests a man using a scythe. African Spoonbills have lilac-coloured bills and pink feet. European Spoonbills have black bills and black feet; they also grow small white crests on their heads during the breeding season.

Ibises also resemble storks but have relatively shorter legs and are not much larger than farmyard hens. They have long slender bills which have a very obvious downward curve. Ibises of one kind or another live in most of the world's warmer countries, two of the four East African species being among the commoner birds in the National Parks. One of these is the Sacred Ibis, which shares the swampy island with the herons. The other is the Hagerdash Ibis which you also see in swampy backwaters of the Nile.

Sacred Ibises are very striking birds with pure white plumage which contrasts superbly with the black of their naked heads and necks, and of their bushy tails. They add greatly to the beauty of the Nile, particularly when they fly low over the water in formation, with their white wings showing a decorative black hem. As you watch these birds you are constantly aware of their delicate appearance. In flight they seem to stroke the air, and the slow beat of their wings is usually interspersed with periods of sailing. It is an action which contrasts completely with the purposeful flight of the Spur-winged Geese which are often in the air at the same time. 'Spur-wings', Africa's largest geese, are a familiar sight on the Nile as they fly up and down the river at dawn and dusk.

The Sacred Ibis is called 'sacred' because it was worshipped in ancient Egypt, though it is almost extinct in that country today. The Egyptians believed that the bird itself was divine, and that it served as scribe to Osiris, great god of the Nile, recording the life of every individual man and woman. The Egyptians used to watch the Ibises probing into the soft mud beside the river as they searched for food with their long bills. This action, by suggesting that the birds were writing, seems to have been the origin of this strange belief. Ibises were mummified when they died, and were buried in temples with the Pharaohs. Weird beings, with human bodies and ibis heads, were often depicted on Egyptian carvings.

The Hagerdash Ibis is frequently called 'Hadada' because of

its mournful cry which is one of the most familiar African sounds: 'ha-da-da, ha-da-da', starting on a high note and ending on a low note. It is a glossy, dark green and brown bird which stands about two feet high. Though you often find Hadadas beside the Nile, they really prefer smaller wooded streams and little pools, so that you may see them wherever there is standing water, even on wayside ponds and ditches.

Herons and ibises are not the only birds that indulge in colonial nesting on this fascinating stretch of the Nile. Pied Kingfishers and Red-throated Bee-eaters have established an entirely different type of colony. For the most part, the banks of the river are low or broken. At one point, however, a steep sandstone cliff drops about thirty feet into deep water. This cliff is riddled with hundreds of small round holes, and I have often sat in a boat at its base, watching spellbound as the kingfishers and bee-eaters fly in and out of the holes and go about their business. This colony is used by many more kingfishers than nest in any single cliff beside the Kazinga Channel where suitable nesting cliffs or banks are much more plentiful. The bee-eaters, moreover, provide a wonderful splash of colour in this Nile-side colony.

Ten different kinds of bee-eater, which are among the most vividly coloured of all birds, have been seen in the Uganda National Parks. They vary in length from about six to almost twelve inches, and many species have very long tail feathers. All have compact, streamlined bodies and long, sharp, curved bills. Most kinds of bee-eater are predominantly green in colour with brilliant yellow, red, blue or black splashes in their plumage. They are not water birds, but often hawk for insects above water and sometimes actually dive.

Bee-eaters make nests rather like those of kingfishers. Beside the Nile, you see the Red-throated Bee-eaters flying at the cliff, which they strike with their bills. Sometimes they fly rapidly backwards and forwards from a distance of two feet or less. Occasionally they work more slowly from further off. They bore out downward-sloping tunnels which may be as much as four or five feet deep. These end in small nesting chambers and are usually well lined with the wings of bees and the other flying insects that these birds eat. There is always intense activity at such nesting places whenever bee-eaters are breeding. These spectacular birds seem constantly to be boring out new holes or carrying insects to their nestlings hidden away in the cliff.

The Whale-headed Stork, or Shoe-bill, is perhaps the most extraordinary of all the birds that you are likely to see by the Nile. Shoe-bills are huge, heavy, rather grotesque-looking birds that stand well over three feet tall. They are greenish-grey in colour, so that they match their surroundings perfectly. They have enormous bills which are about eight inches in length and are shaped like shoes that are almost as broad as they are long. This remarkable bill is armed with a formidable hook, like the hook on a cormorant's bill on a larger scale, which is useful for digging out and grasping the buried frogs and mud-fish which form a considerable part of the Shoe-bill's diet.

Shoe-bills are morose, solitary birds. They spend most of the day hidden in papyrus swamps, or reed-beds, only emerging to feed in the cool of the evening. Their great yellow eyes suggest that they can see well in the dark, and this probably is so, because they do much of their hunting at night. Shoe-bills are not exactly rare but you seldom see them, and I always considered myself lucky if I caught sight of one when travelling on the river by boat. You see them occasionally to the landward side of the papyrus swamps, and there are one or two places where there is always a chance of doing this. Shoe-bills stand absolutely still for long periods at a time, with their great bills resting on their chests, when it is difficult to say if they are sleeping, resting or waiting for their prey.

I was once watching a Shoe-bill when it suddenly woke up. It evidently objected to my being there, as it started chattering its bill and then walked slowly in my direction for a few yards before changing its mind and returning to its swamp. I have heard of one walking right up to a stationary car at Buligi where the Nile enters Lake Albert. This Shoe-bill approached at a slow, sedate pace, chattering its bill all the time, and continuing to do this while it walked all round the car which it seemed to examine carefully. After appearing to satisfy itself that the car and its occupants were harmless, the bird stopped its aggressive bill-chattering and walked away. Shoe-bills are not true storks but, like storks, chatter their bills as a form of display, whether they are trying to frighten off an enemy or attract a mate.

4

Birds of the Smaller Lakes and Pools – Flamingoes and Wading Birds

Many thousands of years ago there were violent volcanic eruptions in part of what is now the Queen Elizabeth National Park. This has left an area of about forty square miles deeply pitted with extinct craters, the largest of which is over a mile wide and a thousand feet deep. Most of these craters are covered in forest or grass, and are frequented by the kinds of bird that prefer those habitats. A few hold salty, brackish water, however; and there is so much salt in one of them, the Katwe Salt Lake, that the local people dig it out to sell in commercial quantities. The concentration of salt in the water of all the lakes changes with the seasons and the amount of rainfall. It is generally too salty for fish, so the craters are seldom visited by fish-eating birds. But there are fish in Lake Kikorongo, one of the larger crater lakes, and you can usually see pelicans and Fish Eagles there.

Lake Kikorongo is at the edge of the crater country, close to Lake George from which it is separated by a narrow strip of low-lying land. There are many birds there; and the Uganda kobs, which are particularly attractive antelopes, drink there regularly. The surrounding country is fairly open but a few trees and bushes grow beside the water. You can sit in the shade of these, enjoy the view and watch the animals and birds without disturbing them. I have seldom visited this lake without seeing something interesting.

One day I went to Kikorongo and parked my Land Rover some distance away. I started walking down to the lake but was greeted by a most frightful stench when I was still more than a hundred yards from the water. I expected to find a dead elephant, or that one hippopotamus had killed another in a fight, but soon saw that the lake was lined with dead and dying fish, upon which a number of Marabou Storks were gorging themselves.

I saw no animal tracks on the sandy beach of the lake – the antelopes were evidently drinking elsewhere. There had been no rain for some weeks so that the level of water in the lake was much lower than usual. The obvious explanation was that this, together with evaporation, had caused a rise in the concentration of salt in the water. The lake had become so salty that the fish had died.

A few days afterwards, a flock of over a thousand flamingoes arrived and settled down at the edge of the lake. I have no idea where these flamingoes came from. They had no permanent home in the area, although a few stray birds would appear in the region from time to time. Then they would usually spend a few days, or weeks, on the Katwe Salt Lake. Flamingoes can only live where there is brackish, salty water: they feed almost entirely on minute water-weeds, chiefly algae and microscopic diatoms, which only grow in this sort of water. Although flamingoes had bred on Lake Kikorongo more than fifty years ago, they had not visited it for several years. It is a complete mystery how they discovered that they would find the right kind of food there.

These flamingoes spent nearly a year on the lake. Towards the end of that time, we noticed that some of them were beginning to come into breeding condition. Their plumage became a deeper colour than that of the others, and the birds themselves showed signs of increasing restlessness. Flamingoes display by huddling together, bobbing their heads up and down, and stretching their necks upwards so that their bills point towards the sky. While doing this they constantly move their legs and feet as if jiving to the rhythm of pop music.

It then rained for several days and nothing came of the flamingoes' antics. The rainfall greatly reduced the concentration of salt in the water so that the special water-weeds would not grow. The flamingoes were no longer able to find their own particular food on Lake Kikorongo. Instead of breeding, they left for an unknown destination.

No more flamingoes were seen in the Queen Elizabeth Park for about four years. Then we suddenly saw twelve on a small crater near the Katwe Salt Lake. They were there for a few months and then, quite unexpectedly, a large flock appeared on Lake Kikorongo. Once again they stayed for about a year and disappeared after heavy rain had raised the level of the lake. For part of this time there was also a fair sized flock on another crater lake just outside the park. It is almost impossible to trace out the erratic way in which flamingoes move about East Africa.

The number of flamingoes that appear from time to time in the Queen Elizabeth Park is small compared with the huge flocks you see on the Rift Valley lakes in Kenya and Tanzania. Hundreds of thousands stand closely packed together near the shores of the lakes, giving the whole place a marvellous pink glow. Then something disturbs the flamingoes and they all take off, wheeling round the lake like an animated crimson cloud. This happens at night as well as during the day, and even if you cannot see the birds you can hear their gentle goose-like honking as they call to one another.

Massed flamingoes, whether on the ground or in the water or in the air, form one of the most magnificent wild life spectacles to be seen anywhere in the world. Even the comparatively small flock on Lake Kikorongo took one's breath away. Flamingoes preen and clean themselves a great deal so that their pink and crimson plumage always looks perfectly groomed, even though they spend most of their lives in dirty, smelly water.

Two kinds of flamingoes are found in East Africa: the Lesser and the Greater. Lesser Flamingoes, which are much more numerous, stand about four feet tall. Greater Flamingoes stand about five feet tall but are not so brightly coloured. There are also small differences in the shape and construction of their bills. Generally, however, the two kinds of flamingo look much the same apart from their difference in size, and you usually find them together in the same flocks, a few Greater Flamingoes standing out among the huge mass of Lessers. The birds which came to Kikorongo were all Lesser Flamingoes. There was one Greater, however, among the twelve we found near the Katwe Salt Lake.

Both kinds of flamingo have bills which are specially adapted for extracting algae and diatoms from the water. The inside of the bill is covered with fine hairs arranged in lines. These hairs serve as a filtering device and allow water to pass in and out of the bill while retaining the algae, which are then rolled backwards and forwards on to the tongue. The tongue works like a piston, forcing water through the bill and drawing the algae down the bird's gullet.

You see flamingoes feeding with a swinging motion of their heads and an action, not unlike that of spoonbills, which suggests a man using a scythe. But, when flamingoes feed, they curve their necks to such an extent that their heads are upside down and their lower mandibles uppermost in the water. They usually stand or walk slowly through the shallows, but can feed equally well when swimming in deeper water. They spend most of the night feeding and you sometimes see them out on the lakes early in the mornings. Flamingoes find all their food in the surface layer of the water, so are not able to feed if the lakes are at all rough.

I was very disappointed that the flamingoes did not nest on Lake Kikorongo, as they have quite fascinating nesting habits.

They collect mud in their bills and build it up into little mounds at the edge of the water where it dries hard in the sun. They lay their eggs on top of these mounds, and both parents take turns in sitting on them until they hatch about four weeks later. At first the little flamingoes are covered with soft down and are unable to move. After a few hours, however, they sit up and take notice, and begin to make calls begging for food. After a few days, you see them standing up like young goslings, demanding food from their parents. Unlike most kinds of bird, flamingoes do not breed regularly every year; nor do they have a fixed breeding season. Like their movements from one lake to another, this is part of the mystery which surrounds the life of flamingoes.

Lakes and rivers are not the only places in the National Parks where there is water. There are pools and water-holes throughout the bushland, and these vary in size from small lakes, several hundred yards across, to tiny ponds which only hold water for a few days after heavy rain. Even the largest pools are greatly reduced in size when the rains stop, while some dry up completely. Many animals drink in such places in preference to the larger lakes. Many kinds of bird live there in order to take advantage of the rich plant and insect life that thrives in stagnant, muddy water. There are no fish, of course, so that you do not see the fish-eating birds.

There are two large pools in the part of the Queen Elizabeth National Park known as the Royal Circuit (named after the tour made by Her Majesty the Queen Mother in 1959). They are quite close together and about the same size, roughly four hundred yards long by two hundred yards across. Both pools are visited by the same kinds of animal and bird. The vegetation of the surrounding country is similar: clumps of acacia trees, euphorbia trees, and evergreen shrubs which overhang the water. There are swampy verges, of course, but there is also firm, open ground where you can approach the edge of the water in a Land

Rover. Then you can watch the life of the pools without frightening away the various creatures.

My home in the Queen Elizabeth Park was only a few miles away so I often went to the pools. There were always hippos in the water, sleeping contentedly throughout the day. Occasionally a bull hippo would rouse himself and 'yawn' at another to show off his tusks – this is one of the ways in which these animals demonstrate superiority over their rivals, and the gesture may be likened to the threat-display of certain birds. Elephants sometimes came to the pools to drink; but I used generally to see them browsing among the evergreen shrubs or standing sleepily in the shade of one of the euphorbia trees. Buffaloes and antelopes were always in the neighbourhood and one evening I surprised a lioness drinking with her cubs.

On another occasion, I was watching an eagle circling in the sky when I realized that it was dropping down on to a branch where a five-foot monitor lizard was lying. The lizard reared up suddenly when the eagle's outstretched talons were only a few inches from its back. The eagle changed into reverse and perched on another part of the tree. The monitor resumed its siesta as if nothing had happened. Few eagles will attack such a formidable adversary on purpose, but it is difficult to believe that it could have mistaken a lizard for a branch.

Hammerheads nest in the forks of nearby acacia trees, and you can almost always see these birds beside the pools. A few Wood Ibises are usually there, too. You often see them close to the water, sitting on their heels in the strange attitude occasionally adopted by storks. Black Crakes live in thick bush near the pools, timidly skulking out of sight. They are small and dark, with greenish-yellow bills, and have something of the build and movements of Lily-trotters. Sometimes you see an African Moorhen which is very similar to the familiar British bird but slightly smaller.

You often see a pair of Saddle-bill Storks near the pools. They are magnificent birds, and are both larger and more spectacular than Wood Ibises, their nearest rivals in elegance among African storks. They can be recognized immediately by the bright yellow saddle at the base of their bills, and by the striking black and white and violet colour of their plumage. The bill itself is bright red with a black band round the middle.

Saddle-bill Storks behave rather like Goliath Herons. They stand motionless in shallow water or wait in swampy ground for the chance to strike at lizards, frogs or other small creatures. Goliath Herons themselves seldom visit the pools. They find better fishing in the great lakes. You see spoonbills from time to time, and egrets are almost always there. A few flamingoes appeared occasionally while the large flock was present on Lake Kikorongo, which is only about twelve miles away.

Twelve species of duck have been recorded in the National Parks. They all seem to prefer such places as the pools to the more open water of the great lakes. They are generally safer in the smaller pools, where their food can be found more easily. All kinds of duck live on water-weeds and aquatic insects. Some dive for what they eat. Others collect it from the surface by dabbling in the muddy water.

You probably see the White-faced Tree Ducks more often than any of the other species. They are rather comical-looking ducks, particularly when you see them on the ground. Their white faces and very upright stance give them the appearance of being permanently surprised. When in the water they dive for their food. They have the habit of preening and grooming each other's feathers, and you frequently see them busily employed in this way. They have a slow, rather deliberate flight and, when in the air, call to each other with a low whistling note.

Another duck that you often see is the Red-bill. It is a very well known African bird, but the name is rather confusing – these birds have no connection with American Red-billed Whistling Ducks to which the same name is given. African Red-bills are medium-sized, greyish-coloured ducks which look rather like European Wigeon but have longer tails. They swim with their bodies higher in the water than most ducks, and obtain all their food either by dabbling on the surface or on land. They never dive. Red-bills, like White-faced Tree Ducks, live in Africa throughout the year, so you may see them on the pools at any season. Little Hottentot Teals and African Pochards are often there as well. This Pochard is probably the commonest of all the East African diving ducks. It is a dark brown bird, and the male has a white bar on his wing.

Egyptian Geese also frequent the pools. They are probably more at home there than on the Kazinga Channel, because there are no large fish to worry them. They certainly seem more ready to take to the water; if they are disturbed on the banks they waddle in hurriedly, flapping their wings in their agitation. You do not often see Knob-billed or Spur-winged Geese, which are the most familiar geese in this part of Africa except for the Egyptians. Geese get most of their food by grazing on dry land.

Pigmy Geese appear occasionally. They are beautiful little birds with bright green backs, and heads that are coloured black, white and green in a sharply defined pattern. They are no larger than teal, dive like ducks and perch on trees. They do not walk at all easily and have a quick, twisting flight that is not at all goose-like. They are known as 'geese' because of the shape of their bills, although they are really ducks. They are more closely akin to the Wood Ducks of North America and the Mandarin Ducks which are so well known as ornamental birds in Britain.

The wading birds, or shore birds, are perhaps the most interesting of all those that come to the pools. They wade in the shallows and walk about on marshy ground, probing for worms, water-breeding insects and their larvae. Most kinds of wading

Knob-billed Goose

A Common Sandpiper on its nest

Black-tailed Godwit

bird have rather long, pliable bills and long legs without feathers on their thighs. Their plumage is generally grey, brown or mottled, though many show distinct black and white patches, stripes or bands. They vary in size from the familiar Curlew, the largest of the group, to the Little Stint. You sometimes see them singly, sometimes in flocks, and you often find several different kinds of wader together. They frequent the margins of inland waters and sea-coasts throughout the world. You see them in the National Parks, beside the lakes and rivers and wherever the ground is suitable for them. Nearly all wading birds nest on the ground.

Thirty-eight different species of wading birds, representing four distinct families, have been seen in the National Parks. There are small Ringed Plovers with plump, compact bodies, rather short bills and pointed wings. There are the larger Lapwing Plovers, which have longer legs and broad, rounded wings. Like Ringed Plovers, Lapwings have rather short bills, which is one of the features that enables you to distinguish plovers from most other kinds of wading bird. Lapwings fly in a loose, floppy-looking way, so that you can always recognize them even at a distance.

There are Oystercatchers, Avocets and Stilts, which have long thin legs and exceptionally long bills. Finally, there is the family of the true waders which includes Sandpipers, Godwits, Redshanks, Stints, Ruffs, Curlews and others. As you might expect of such a large family, individual species vary considerably. However, you can always distinguish waders from plovers by the way they move as they search for food. True waders run about with lowered heads probing the ground with their bills. Plovers hold their heads up, stop quickly and then tilt over to seize some morsel that takes their fancy. You see some of these wading birds on the Royal Circuit pools at any time of the year. But the majority, including all the true waders, only visit tropical Africa during the European winter.

5

The commonest of the Lapwings are the Spur-winged Plovers and the Wattled Plovers which have yellow legs and yellow wattles hanging down on either side of their bills. Both these plovers live in the National Parks throughout the year. You often see them on the open grassland, though they seldom go far away from water; in the evenings they frequently come out on to dusty or sandy tracks. Another Lapwing that lives in the area permanently is the Long-toed Plover, which has a white head and white shoulders. It lives on the marshy fringes of lakes and water-holes, and favours places where the Nile cabbages grow.

Two kinds of Ringed Plovers are also present throughout the year. One is the Three-banded Plover, which has distinct black and white bands on his chest. These plovers run about at the edge of the pools or make short sharp flights from one feeding ground to another. They are usually alone or in pairs, and if you frighten one by making a sudden noise, it bobs its head up and down and rocks its tail to show its agitation.

Another Ringed Plover is Kittlitz's Sand Plover, which has no very obvious black and white bands. You frequently see these Sand Plovers near the pools, as a few pairs nest on almost grass-less ground close to the water. If you disturb a Kittlitz's Sand Plover at its nest, it quickly claws dusty soil over the eggs and then staggers away pretending that its wing is broken. By means of this trick, it hopes to call attention to itself and away from its eggs or from its nestlings.

You invariably see Black-winged Stilts at the pools. They are elegantly built, black and white birds with long, straight, black bills. They stand about fourteen inches tall on slender, pink legs. You normally find a pair together and can tell the female from the male by her brownish-coloured head. They walk about slowly in shallow water, searching for tadpoles and aquatic insects. You can usually get quite close to them without difficulty but, like most wading birds, they make a little piping alarm call when frightened.

Black-winged Stilts indulge in a most curious breeding display. The male cries out and staggers around in a drunken sort of way, finally collapsing on to the ground with his wings half-open. But he soon gets up again and then leaps into the air three or four times as if trapped or held by an invisible cord round one leg. Stilts sometimes nest on dry ground but more often do so on floating reeds, rather like Lily-trotters. Two or three nests are usually placed close together.

There is even the chance of seeing a Painted Snipe, a very shy bird indeed. The Painted Snipe is about the same size as the familiar Common Snipe but is more heavily built and brightly coloured. It also has a shorter bill. The Painted Snipe is not nearly so nimble on the wing as the Common Snipe which is famous for its rapid zig-zag flight. With most kinds of bird, if they fight at all, the males fight each other. Painted Snipe, however, behave in exactly the opposite way: the females fight when there is competition over males. The male Painted Snipe prepares the nest, which is little more than a hollow in the grass or rushes. In due course he also incubates the eggs and rears the young. The female just lays her eggs and then goes off to look for another male. She mates with him and lays some more eggs. Once again she leaves her mate to sit on the eggs alone, while she wanders off.

All these birds may be seen at the Royal Circuit pools and other suitable places in the National Parks throughout the year. They are the only birds present between April and September. But towards the end of September, the scene changes. Familiar birds, which have been missing for the past six months, begin to re-appear. Both the number and variety of birds is increased enormously as migrants from the north reach the National Parks. For the next six or seven months you may see almost any of the northern waders as well as birds of many other kinds. They have

travelled thousands of miles to get there and may stay for only a
few hours, or days, before moving on. Others remain for weeks
or even throughout the European winter season. This is part of
the annual bird migration: the regular movement of certain species
from one area, in which they breed, to another where they spend
part of the year.

Migration is one of the least understood aspects of bird behaviour. The places from which the migrants start their journeys,
and where these end, are known for many species; but we are
only now beginning to find out full details of the routes followed.
We cannot yet explain completely how birds find their way, how
they manage to visit the same places year after year, or what
makes them start. It is almost certain, even so, that migrating
birds navigate by the sun during the day-time and by the stars at
night. Some, but certainly not the majority, may follow natural
features such as rivers or sea coasts. They usually seem to start
their journeys in calm weather and under a clear sky; and they
sometimes fly above low clouds to keep the stars in view. When
it is misty, or when the rain clouds are heavy, the birds usually
drop down to earth to rest and feed. They are marvellously
clever at finding the best and most direct routes. But how they
do this remains largely a mystery.

Some kinds of bird fly thousands of miles without rest or food.
Others rest frequently. Some travel by day. Others travel by
night, among them species which are normally active only during
the day-time. Certain kinds of bird fly alone or in small groups.
Others move in huge flocks. When migrating, birds generally
fly higher over the sea than over land except when forced upwards by such obstacles as mountain ranges. They tend also to
fly higher at night than during the day.

Migrants include huge birds, such as cranes and storks, and
quite small birds such as Little Stints, swallows, warblers and
even tiny humming-birds. You cannot help being surprised that

small birds, in particular, should be able to travel these enormous distances. In fact, however, many species normally fly a remarkably long way in their daily search for food. The Common Swift, for example, is believed to fly six hundred miles or more, almost every day of its life, while collecting and eating insects. Such birds as starlings frequently cover sixty or seventy miles. Many kinds of bird are evidently capable of flying from Europe to the tropics in a reasonably short time without travelling very much further than they normally do when not migrating.

The main reasons for these regular journeys is food. Insects, which many birds eat, are abundant in the far North and plentiful throughout Europe during the summer. But when the cold winter weather arrives, and with it the long northern nights, conditions become impossible. Few birds can then survive at all in the Arctic; and there is little insect-food anywhere in Europe or Northern Asia. In the tropics food is plentiful all the year round, and there is never any serious shortage of insects. There is sufficient for the resident birds and for those that travel from the north. But birds of prey, flesh-eating animals and snakes are also plentiful. There are great dangers for nesting birds, particularly those that make poor nests or which nest on the ground as do most of the waders. So it is not surprising that insect-eating birds and wading birds should prefer to breed in Europe and the North, and that they should then seek a better climate with a richer supply of the foods they eat.

By travelling from one part of the world to another certain kinds of bird are able to find the best conditions for living throughout the year. The advantage of this evidently makes the hazards worth while. The journeys themselves are both exhausting and dangerous, of course, particularly when severe winds blow birds off their normal course. Many migrating birds fail to reach their destination.

The problems of bird migration are still being studied by

ornithologists. For many years the chief method of study has been ringing: catching birds, often at their nests, marking them by placing numbered rings on their legs, and noting the details from the rings which happen to be found in other countries. Workers in many different countries assist one another in this study, from which the distances travelled and the routes followed can be learnt. In addition to ringing, ornithologists are now using radar to find out exactly what happens on the actual flights. The movement of flocks of birds can be watched and recorded from as far away as ninety miles with the help of special radar installations. It is even possible, under certain conditions, to watch, on a radar screen, the flight of an individual bird and to measure the speed at which it travels.

The waders are a most striking example of a whole group of birds whose lives are dominated by migration. The snipe and sandpipers that you see in the National Parks breed and spend the summer months in northern Europe, northern Asia or the Arctic. They fly out to Africa each year in the autumn and return to the north in the spring. Some fly across or round the Mediterranean. Others traverse the Middle East on their way to Africa. Most of those that come to the National Parks probably then follow the River Nile. They seem generally to use the same routes year after year.

A number of birds ringed in Europe have been recovered in Uganda and elsewhere in East Africa. The rings have shown that most of the birds concerned came from Denmark, Finland, Germany, Poland or Russia. No bird ringed in Britain, where ringing is carried out at several observatories, has yet been recovered in Uganda. British migrants go to West Africa. Many of the waders that you see in the National Parks are of the same species as those found in Britain, although the individual birds come from further east. For example, no Dunlin, which is one of Britain's commonest small waders, has yet been observed in the National Parks. Dunlins migrate to other parts of Africa. The Common Sandpiper of Britain also occurs in north-eastern Europe and Siberia. This species is seen quite often in the National Parks but Marsh Sandpipers are very much more common. Marsh Sandpipers are rarely seen in Britain. They are east European birds.

Arrival of the migrants changes the whole character of such places as the Royal Circuit pools. Some migrants stay in the area for the whole season. Others move on to southern Africa, where they find conditions that may be even more suitable to them. You usually see more than one kind of Sandpiper, Little Stints, Ringed Plovers and perhaps a Redshank. Both Curlew Sandpipers and Wood Sandpipers are often there, sometimes congregating in quite large flocks particularly where the ground is flooded. Ruffs and Greenshanks are nearly always present. Snipe rise noisily from the reed patches as you approach. You do not know what bird you may see at the pools, and this certainly adds interest to every visit.

Occasionally there is the excitement of a rare bird, such as the Bar-tailed or Black-tailed Godwits. Dusky Spotted Redshanks appear fairly regularly. Curlews, Avocets and Oystercatchers are sometimes seen; they are common enough in Europe, of course, but rarities in the heart of Africa. But the greatest rarity was the Grey Phalarope which a friend of mine saw and photographed while it was resting on the water. These small grey waders migrate from the Arctic and hardly ever leave the sea coasts. No Grey Phalarope had been seen before within hundreds of miles of the Queen Elizabeth Park. This solitary bird was a thousand miles away from its normal winter home on the Indian Ocean.

Six of the twelve species of duck seen in the National Parks are migrants. They appear on the pools at the same time as the waders. You see flocks of Garganey and Pintail at the edge of the pools, dabbling for water-weeds in the shallows. Garganey are small and greyish in colour. Their flight is fast and agile. They breed in Britain occasionally, but their main breeding grounds are further east. The Garganey that winter in the Queen Elizabeth Park probably come from Finland or Asiatic Russia. Pintails, with their long tails and long necks, are also well known in Britain but, again, British Pintails do not visit the National Parks. Other species of duck, which are familiar in Europe, also visit the pools. Shovelers, with their bright colours and wide bills, come to East Africa from arctic Russia by way of the Caspian Sea. A few pairs of Teal join the Hottentot Teal that are already there. European Pochards appear sometimes and can be distinguished from African Pochards because the drake is much lighter in colour.

These migrant birds usually seem to arrive singly in the autumn. They often look tired and dejected for their first few days in their new surroundings. In the spring you see them feeding hungrily to build up reserves of fat for the hardships of their long flight back to their breeding grounds. You frequently see mixed flocks of waders at this season when they collect together for their journey to the north. Many of them will soon be laying and incubating their eggs on a northern bog, or estuary, or even in the arctic tundra.

But you do not see these northern visitors in their full summer breeding plumage. Nor do you see anything of their breeding behaviour which, in some species, is full of interest. However, you may see changes beginning to appear in the plumage of some of these birds. At the beginning of May I have seen a Curlew Sandpiper with its back turning from grey to chestnut, and a Marsh Sandpiper that was developing dark spots on its chest and rump.

Of course, the Royal Circuit pools in the Queen Elizabeth Park are not the only places where ducks and waders are to be seen. There are many similar places in both National Parks, including swampy backwaters of the Nile. I have seen most of these migrants on or near Lake Kikorongo where I once saw five different kinds of duck together.

Ducks and waders are by no means the only migrants to visit the National Parks. Many others appear in the open bush and grasslands. You see doves, wagtails, wheatears, warblers, swallows and other familiar British species though these too come from further east – the Nightingale has been seen a few times in the Murchison Falls Park. These and other well known birds, so typical of the European summer, simply could not exist if Africa did not provide them with a winter home. Many millions of birds undertake these long journeys every year.

Bird migrations do not always involve long journeys from northern Europe or the Arctic to the tropics. Some species move from one part of Africa to another. In the tropics, it is quite usual for birds to follow the rains in their seasonal movements; and this usually means migrating from north to south across the equator and back again. For example, there are certain species of bee-eater, cuckoo and kingfisher which breed in the Sudan and then fly south to avoid the hot, dry weather. As with the long-distance migrants, most of these birds are insect-eaters. A few species from the island of Madagascar may fly across to the mainland of Africa when they have finished breeding. Among these are the colourful Madagascar Bee-eaters which you often see in the Queen Elizabeth Park between May and September. But we do not know for certain that these particular birds have actually crossed the ocean as this species also nests on the mainland near the East African coast. Again birds which live on the flowers or fruits of a small number of plants or trees have to travel to find these special plants in season.

One evening in the late summer, while I was working on this chapter at my home in Cornwall, I went for a walk along the sea-shore. I saw a Redshank and a little flock of Turnstones which were busily looking for insects under pebbles on the beach. These dumpy, medium-sized waders were probably on their way from Iceland to West Africa. I have seen Turnstones behaving in exactly the same way in the Queen Elizabeth Park, turning up stones on a beach beside Lake Edward. I have also seen Redshanks there, but less frequently than the Dusky Spotted Redshank which is not often seen in Britain.

Waders are the outstanding example of a whole group of birds that migrate long distances each year. Whether you see them on the coasts of Britain, or alongside the Royal Circuit pools, they demonstrate one of the most fascinating aspects of bird behaviour.

5

Forest and Woodland Birds

Nearly every kind of bird is able to make a number of different sounds. These are mostly produced by the voice, when they are described as calls or songs, but are sometimes made by other means such as wing-flapping or bill-clattering. Almost every species produces its own particular range of sounds and, as we all know, some bird-songs are both musical and beautiful. Every song, or other sound, has a meaning which is understood by other birds of the same species and, in certain special cases, by birds of other species. So bird-song is a very simple form of language. It enables birds to give information to each other on a strictly limited range of subjects.

Birds call during the breeding season to find, identify and make contact with their mates. Many male birds call with great vigour at this time to proclaim their breeding grounds, or territories, and to threaten other male birds of their own species and tell them to keep away. This is the kind of bird-song which you hear most frequently. This is what is happening on a spring morning in Britain when you hear birds singing in the garden. Some kinds of bird have special calls to announce that a nest has been made, or that it is time for the male and female birds to change over duties at the nest.

A bird's territory is the area in which the individual male bird is master. He mates in his territory and it is where his young will be brought up. He attacks, or at least threatens other males of his own species if they dare to trespass. The songs he sings on his territory are usually loud and distinctive, and they serve to make the singer as conspicuous as possible to other birds of his own species. This kind of territory is held only during the breeding season. With some species, however, territories are held by the females, or by the family, or even by a whole group of birds of the same species particularly those which nest in colonies. Certain species use their territories all the year round. Sometimes territories are held for the purpose of feeding and have nothing to do with mating. The hunting ground of an eagle is an example.

Territories vary enormously in size and, in general, are defended only against birds of the same species. An eagle, which eats rats and mice, does not object to a pigeon eating fruit or a little finch collecting grass-seeds in his hunting territory. Most territory-holders will try to drive away a predator, however, even if it is of another species.

Most kinds of bird have one or more alarm calls which they use at the approach of danger. To most birds danger means that a predator has been observed, and predators generally are of two kinds: animals, such as cats or even humans that move about on the ground and may climb trees; and birds of prey that attack from the air. Different tactics are needed to escape from these dangers. A ground predator is best avoided by taking to the air. A bird of prey can often be driven away by means of collective action, usually described as mobbing, when a number of birds join together to chase the intruder. You frequently see this happening, of course; mobbing can also be effective against enemies on the ground.

Alternatively, dangers from both ground and air can often be avoided by seeking cover and hiding. So, many species have developed alarm calls which tell other birds whether to fly away, hide, or collect together for the purpose of mobbing the enemy. These calls are intended as messages to other members of the same species; but it is useful for all birds in the neighbourhood to know that a danger has been observed.

Again, birds call to keep in touch with one another. You hear this when ducks and geese whistle or honk as they fly, when a flock of migrating birds passes overhead at night, or when a group of little finches is twittering away while feeding on the ground. Birds call to let their nestlings know where they are. In the same way, a nesting pair keeps in touch by calling to each other.

Birds generally have very good eye-sight, and some have conspicuous, brightly coloured plumage. Colours, like songs and calls, help birds to keep in touch and identify one another. They also play their part in breeding behaviour. Male birds of many kinds attract their mates by the display of brightly coloured feathers and use these to threaten and frighten away intruders. Only a few birds, such as owls and nightjars, are active at night when colours do not show up. The great majority feed and move about during the day when they can see well. This being so, why should birds also sing and have a more elaborate system of communication by voice than any other animals except man and a very few others?

The obvious answer is, first, that birds have remarkable powers of flight and frequently travel long distances. They must be able to communicate with each other when they are out of sight – particularly as birds can very easily get separated by accident. Secondly, many kinds of bird are active in dense cover. They can only use sound to keep in touch. So they call or make some other kind of noise, as woodpeckers do when they drum and hammer on trees with their bills. For this reason, you usually find that those birds which live in woods and forests, or which spend the greater part of their lives in thickets or very tall grass, sing most loudly and vigorously. Moreover, some of these birds do not come together just for the breeding season but remain paired for the whole year. It is particularly important that they should have distinct calls, so that there is no danger of the two partners losing one another.

The high evergreen tropical forests of Africa are much more luxuriant than the woods and forests of Europe. They tend, moreover, to be damp and steamy and, for this reason, are known as 'rain forests' in districts where the rainfall is heavy. Innumerable different kinds of tree grow together in great profusion. These vary in height from forest giants, such as mahogany and ironwood which grow to well over a hundred feet, to low-growing shrubs and bushes. There are also smaller trees whose leafy tops never see the sunlight. Known as under-storey trees, these form a half-way stage between the giants and the woody undergrowth, which is often so thick that you can hardly move except along paths or animal tracks. Woody creepers envelop many of the trees, and there is an amazingly rich growth of leaves which lasts throughout the year. Tree orchids, ferns and mosses grow on the trunks and branches. Where the forest is more open, the ground is covered with small plants. Birds of many different kinds stay permanently in these forests which they very seldom leave. Birds from other habitats rarely enter an evergreen forest. The fruits, nuts and seeds produced by the forest trees provide food for many birds, although they may have to move from one part of the forest to another to find trees in the right state of growth. Pigeons are a good example of this.

Another important source of food is the large number of insects. Many birds feed on ants, which mostly live on the ground, and you find these birds wherever the ants are plentiful. Many kinds of bird like to eat caterpillars and to collect them to feed their young. Other birds again inspect cracks and crevices in the bark of trees for grubs and insects. Holes and cavities, abandoned at the end of the nesting season, are often taken over by bees. Later on, other birds appear and eat both the bees and the honey.

Forest birds generally seem to make their nests with particular care. This is largely because of the many small predators that live in the forests. A number of these – the genet cat, for example

– climb trees. Certain birds of prey are also found in the forests. Both sparrowhawks and goshawks hunt and eat other birds, though these do not make up the whole of their diet. Fortunately the great Crowned Eagle, which also lives in forest country, is not normally a bird-eater. Most monkeys eat fruit and leaves but will also take eggs if they chance to find them.

The largest of the forests in the National Parks is the Marama-gambo in the Queen Elizabeth Park. At one time this was joined to the great equatorial forest of the Congo, and you find several species of bird not found anywhere else in what is usually known as East Africa. There are other smaller forests in both Parks, and forest grows along the banks of rivers such as the Chambura and Ishasha in the Queen Elizabeth Park and the several tributaries of the Nile. There are also patches of thick thorn-scrub and large areas of open woodland where the trees grow in long grass and usually lose their leaves during the dry season. These woods, which are quite distinct from the evergreen forests, are visited by many grassland animals in search of shade. They are sometimes ravaged by bush fires. A few forest-loving birds live in the thicker parts of these woodlands.

Different kinds of forest and woodland birds tend to live at different levels. The sun shines most fiercely and the rain beats most violently at the tops of the taller trees. Here there is a plentiful supply of fruits for birds to eat, and the flowers of the trees themselves make this the most colourful part of the forest. You find brightly coloured birds at this level, their colours probably acting as a camouflage. Many of these birds are of large size: turacos, hornbills and parrots for example. There are also smaller birds such as trogons, white-eyes and certain flycatchers. At this tree-top level there are often mixed parties of several species together.

You find a different range of birds living in the under-storey trees: barbets and pigeons are among them. Then there are different birds again on the forest floor where there is little light, what there is giving the ground a speckled look. The birds here tend to be inconspicuous and to have rather dull colouring.

It is difficult to see birds in the forest. Forest-living species are, on the whole, much less well known than those which live in more open country. This is not only because observers find the foliage so thick. It can be extremely dangerous to wander about in country where you may run into a sleeping buffalo or suddenly find yourself only a few feet away from an elephant. Fortunately, however, you can see quite well where roads and tracks cut their way through the forests. Forest verges, too, are favoured by many birds and are easily approached. There is more light, and this means that there is a thick growth of creepers and dense undergrowth with the big trees standing out clearly. You see all the different forest levels at the same time. So you often get a sight of several different kinds of bird, as well as the monkeys which share the trees with them.

The large forest hornbills and turacos often come to these forest verges. Early in the mornings and late in the evenings, parrots fly from one part of the forest to another, screeching at the top of their voices. Birds of many kinds move out to feed on flying insects in the sunlight. At dusk each day when most birds are going to their evening roosts, hundred of bats leave theirs. Very few birds are able to catch a bat on the wing, and very few try to do so. But the Bat-eating Buzzard, or Bat-hawk, eats hardly anything except bats. This bird, which looks like a very much darker form of the familiar European Buzzard, spends the day sitting on a bough in dense forest shade, only coming out for an hour or two in the evenings to hunt for bats. It is seldom seen. Most birds of prey eat on the ground or on a perch. The Bat-hawk holds its prey in its claws and feeds as it flies.

Turacos are probably the most striking birds in the forest. They are large birds, up to thirty inches long, with crests on their

Ground Hornbill

Squacco Heron

Paradise Flycatcher at nest

heads and magnificently bright colours. You often see the Great Blue Turaco, the largest of them, as you drive along the road which passes through the Maramagambo forest. Its plumage is blue, with some green and chestnut, and it has a yellow bill, tipped with red. Another, quite often seen, is Ross's Turaco, which is even more beautiful than the Great Blue as it is coloured blue-black and violet with crimson wings.

In spite of their bright colouring, turacos are not always easy to see in the forest and can be mistaken for flowers or highly coloured leaves. They eat fruit and nest high up in fruit-trees. Turacos rarely descend to the ground, but you sometimes see them gliding from one tree to another across a forest clearing. They are poor fliers but clamber about among the branches like squirrels, being helped in this by the arrangement of their toes. Most birds have the outer toe fixed in position; with turacos this toe can be moved backwards or forwards as required. Some other forest birds also have unusual feet. Woodpeckers, barbets and cuckoos have two toes pointing forwards and two pointing backwards, an arrangement which helps them to grip trees and branches.

As well as being colourful, turacos are exceptionally noisy. Their harsh calls are unmistakable. The Great Blue Turaco starts with a series of rather plaintive notes which gradually deepen into an explosive 'Kok-kok-kok' and end up 'Kurruk-kurruk-kurruk'. Plantain-eaters, grey birds with yellow bills, are members of the same family but live in more open woodland where you often see them flying in single file from one tree to another. Their call is a sort of cackling laugh, and the Acholi people of North Uganda, who always name birds according to their calls and songs, speak of the Grey Plantain-eater as *Okako-kako-kako*, which is exactly the sound it makes. Plantain-eaters are common in the Murchison Falls Park, but the famous Go-away-bird, another member of the same family, lives only in thorn-scrub country further north and

6

east. When a hunter appears and begins a stalk, the Go-away-bird starts bleating like a sheep and warns every animal within miles. Thousands of game animals have been saved by the Go-away-bird which is an outstanding example of a bird whose call helps other species.

Many different kinds of pigeon, dove, cuckoo and woodpecker live in the woods and forests, behaving in much the same way as their relatives do in Europe. Green Pigeons are as common in Africa as Wood Pigeons are in parts of Europe. Like many other birds they are extremely partial to wild figs. Most of the smaller doves, such as the Ring-necked and Mourning Doves, eat the seeds of grass and weeds, so that they are more at home in open woodland country than in true forest. However, the little brown Tambourine Dove and the Western Lemon Dove both live in forests and usually feed on the ground. These Lemon Doves tend to be rather shy. But when one, which had damaged itself, flew into my sitting-room in the Queen Elizabeth Park, it allowed itself to be caught quite easily. We treated its wound and fed it; soon it was able to fly away.

Pigeons and doves are not always as gentle as they are popularly supposed to be. You often see them attacking one another, particularly when the males are defending their territories during the mating season. They mostly make rather skimpy nests in which both parents help to incubate the eggs and feed the young birds. The young pigeon puts its bill into its parent's mouth and drinks the 'pigeon's milk', a cheese-like substance which forms in the crop of the parent pigeon.

European Cuckoos migrate to Africa where they join a number of other kinds of cuckoo which live in Africa all the year round. In doing so, they demonstrate one of the most remarkable features of migration: the ability of birds to find their own way over enormous distances. Cuckoos, as is well known, lay their eggs in the nests of other birds which then incubate them and take care of the nestlings. Adult Cuckoos take no part in the upbringing of their own young which they never see. They also start their migrations about a month before the young birds which are not then even ready to fly. But as soon as they are able to do so, the young Cuckoos set out for their winter quarters in Africa, getting there without guidance and without mistake. They stay in open woodlands rather than in thick evergreen forests – very few forest species are long distance migrants.

Most kinds of cuckoo have the same breeding habits as the European Cuckoo. They mostly have distinctive calls though these are not the same as the familiar 'cuck-coo' we hear in Europe. One of the most beautiful of the African cuckoos is the Emerald Cuckoo, a lovely green and gold bird which lives high up in the forest trees. They are not easy to find, but you sometimes see one at the edge of a forest belt or beside a wooded stream. Another fine bird is the Didric Cuckoo which is bottle-green and bronze in colour. It lives in open country and is the cuckoo most often seen in the Parks. Didric Cuckoos often lay their eggs on the ground and carry them in their bills to the chosen nest. Like most kinds of cuckoo, they eat a large number of caterpillars.

Coucals, long-tailed birds whose most obvious colouring is black and chestnut, belong to the same family as cuckoos but have very different habits. They make their own nests. They have a slow, rather awkward flight, and you often see them creeping about in low-growing bushes, or in forest clearings, where they feed on large insects. The White-browed Coucals are those most often seen in the Parks. They are sometimes called 'Water-bottle Birds' because their bubbling calls sound rather like water being poured out of a bottle.

Eight different kinds of woodpecker have been seen in the Parks. Some live in the depths of the forest: for example the Brown-eared and Yellow-crested Woodpeckers. Others live in more open country. They all behave in much the same way, with habits similar to those of the familiar European Woodpeckers. They cling to tree-trunks, using their tails for support, and feed mainly on insects and grubs that they find in the bark. They dig into this with their powerful chisel-shaped bills and probe with their long barbed tongues. A pair of Little Spotted Woodpeckers once nested in a hole in a euphorbia tree in the grounds of the Mweya Safari Lodge. They were not at all shy and paid no attention when a washing line was tied to the tree just above their nest. These woodpeckers sometimes feed on white ants on the ground.

If you walk along a game track beside the wooded Chambura River, you may see a Giant Kingfisher or hear its cackling laugh. These kingfishers, which are rather larger than jackdaws, are something like Pied Kingfishers in colour. They do not hover but usually sit on a bough above the water waiting for the chance to dive for fish or crabs. In the same sort of place you may also see the Shining Blue Kingfisher, which is probably the most beautiful of all the many African kingfishers.

Not all kingfishers eat fish. Several species feed largely on insects. The forest-loving Blue-breasted Kingfisher, dark grey and blue with a long blue tail, does so. It nests in trees and sometimes bores out a hole in an old nest of tree-ants (arboreal termites) which looks rather like a huge oak-apple gall. But the insect-eating kingfisher you see most often is the Grey-headed Kingfisher. It is a lovely bird and there was nearly always a pair in my garden at Mweya. They sat on the garden fence or darted from one post to another. I remember one trying to kill a small lizard by repeatedly banging its head on a post.

There is the possibility of seeing the rare Finfoot in one of the wooded streams. Finfoots are extraordinary birds, something like moorhens with plumage that is pale brown with some black, white and green. They also have bright orange bills and feet with fringed toes. The Finfoot is not easy to see as it swims rather low in the water and usually stays near overgrown banks where it feeds on insects taken from the surface. Finfoots do not dive. If disturbed, they patter along the surface of the water with beating wings and make for land where they clamber about on fallen branches or among the thick riverside vegetation. They have a strong sense of territory, and a pair seems to spend its whole life on one short stretch of river. If you have once succeeded in locating a Finfoot, you can nearly always find it again in the same place.

The Grey Parrot, so familiar as a household pet and mimic, lives in these forests. So does the little Red-headed Lovebird, which is also a kind of parrot. Like the Blue-breasted Kingfisher, it nests in holes dug out of the tree-ant's nests. Most kinds of parrot are brightly coloured, noisy, screeching birds which live in the tree-tops, flying fast and straight as a bullet. They leave the forests at times, particularly when grain crops are ripening: they are very partial to grain although they feed mainly on fruit.

Barbets also eat fruit and seeds which they crush with their heavy bills. They are true forest birds and share some of the habits of both parrots and woodpeckers. They are noisy and boldly coloured. The larger barbets are nine or ten inches long; the smaller species, known as tinker birds, are only about four inches. They all have little tufts of feather growing around their nostrils; and some species, including the Double-toothed Barbet, have notched bills. The little Lemon-rumped Tinker-bird is one of the noisiest. It makes a series of pops, like a hammer beating on metal, and continues to do this for up to half an hour without stopping.

Another unusual forest bird is Narina's Trogon. In spite of its conspicuous green, blue and red colouring, you seldom see this little bird. It spends most of the day sitting on a bough, high up among the evergreen forest trees. Trogons swoop for insects, which they take on the wing like flycatchers, and they have a monotonous, booming call. Trogons do not migrate, but they sometimes leave their forests and seem to travel more than most forest species.

There are thousands of small birds in the forests, mostly warblers, flycatchers, bulbuls, babblers and white-eyes. Nearly all are rather dull in colour and they would be difficult to tell apart if it were not for their calls; the majority are outstandingly good songsters. Warblers and flycatchers are well known in Britain, of course, and some of the warblers that you see in East Africa are winter visitors from Europe. The small Willow Warbler, for instance, is familiar in Britain and is widely distributed in European woodlands during the summer. It is also found in large numbers near the forest verges in the National Parks between October and March.

Nearly all the many different kinds of warbler seen in the Parks are small greenish-coloured birds which live in trees, shrubs, reeds or grass. You see them moving about among the foliage, looking for grubs and insects. Most of them sing striking songs, particularly when proclaiming their territories. The forest warbler seen most often is the Fan-tailed Warbler. You usually find little parties of four or five together in the undergrowth close to forest streams, The Buff-bellied Warbler stays almost exclusively in the tree-tops and prefers more open woodland to thick forest. The little Crombecs, with stumpy tails and curved bills, search for insects along the boughs of trees at the edge of the forest.

Not all warblers live in woods or forests. Cisticolas, in particular, stay in the open grassland. The Zitting Cisticola, so called because of its 'zitting' call, is one of the commonest. It makes its nest of soft grass, bound together with cobwebs and attached to thicker stems of grass, about twelve or eighteen inches above ground level. Most other kinds of warbler make purse-like nests which you see hanging from branches.

Wherever there are trees, there seem to be flycatchers. The habitat which suits them best, however, is forest and woodland clearings. Twenty-one species of flycatcher have been recorded in the Parks alone, compared to the five known to occur in the whole of Europe. All are small birds with flat bills surrounded by little bristles. They tend to sit very still and straight upright on any convenient perch, usually on one of the smaller branches of a tall tree. From such a perch the flycatcher sees well and will dart off suddenly to chase a passing insect, nearly always returning to the same perch.

Most of the flycatchers that you see in the Parks live there all the year round. But the Spotted Flycatcher is a migrant from Europe. You can recognize it by its habit of flicking its wings as it sits on its perch, which is usually a bare bough at the edge of a wood. Dusky Flycatchers look much the same, but perch on low-growing bushes and sometimes even hawk insects from the ground. They lay their eggs in nests deserted by other birds. Most kinds of flycatcher make their own cup-shaped nests of twigs and moss bound together by cobwebs, and you see these tucked into the forks of moderate-sized trees.

Paradise Flycatchers are the most spectacular African members of this family. They are coloured grey, black and chestnut, and the central tail feathers of the male are twice the length of the bird's body. As you watch these lovely little birds, they seem to be flying around trailing long trains behind them. They are brave as well as beautiful and attack or threaten any bird of prey that comes too close.

You find babblers near the forest edge, moving about on the ground or in low-growing trees or shrubs. Their colouring is generally dull, and they have thickish bills, rather long tails and short rounded wings. Babblers stay together in small flocks and make a great deal of noise as they flit from bush to bush in their slightly awkward way. They hardly ever come out into the open except during the breeding season.

Of the other forest birds, bulbuls and greenbuls are the commonest. The best known member of this large family is the Dark-capped Bulbul which you seem to see everywhere. These bulbuls are widespread in wooded country and you find them in gardens as well as in the wilds. They are coloured mouse-brown with black heads and white bellies, and always seem to be singing cheerfully. *Bulbul* is an old Arabic word. It was used by the poet Omar Khayyám and, in the well-known English version of the *Rubaiyat*, has been translated 'Nightingale', an entirely different kind of bird but a world-famous songster. The original 'Eastern Nightingale' was probably the White-cheeked Bulbul of Pakistan and the Middle East, a close relative of African bulbuls.

Bulbuls have the habit of collecting together in little flocks to mob any snake or predatory animal that comes too close. There are several kinds of bulbul, but most of them live in the depths of the forest so that they are seldom seen. They eat fruit, berries and sometimes also insects.

You see White-browed Robin-chats at the edge of the forest. These handsome birds, related to the thrush, are good songsters, too. They are also excellent mimics, often imitating the calls of other birds such as cuckoos and sometimes even eagles. They spend most of their time on the ground and, like bulbuls, frequently come into gardens. The Green White-eyes, which look rather like warblers but have a ring of white feathers round their eyes, behave very differently. They live in the leafy tree-tops and, except during the breeding season, stay together in flocks. You hear them twittering away as they search the trees for insects and small fruits.

There are also hornbills in the forests, and they make an extraordinary contrast to these little birds. There are several different kinds of hornbill, but they are all large, ungainly birds with enormous, highly coloured bills. The bills of many of the hornbills are enlarged by an extra piece on top, known as a casque, and this gives the birds a slightly absurd appearance. Their plumage is generally black, white and brown. All the hornbills are noisy birds. They fly rather awkwardly but manage to scramble about among the branches in quite an agile way. Their main food is fruit and berries, though they also eat insects and small animals at times. Hornbills are believed to have feeding territories, the same pair of hornbills using the same territory for several years.

Three species of hornbill live in the woods and forests of the Parks. The Black and White Casqued Hornbills, nearly three feet long, normally stay in thick forest. Sometimes, however, they come out into the open to feed on bananas to which they seem particularly partial; and you quite often see them flying across forest clearings. They are very noisy in the air. Not only does the passage of air through their wing-feathers produce a sound like a puffing railway engine, but they scream as if trying to make themselves as conspicuous as possible. Crowned Hornbills are smaller and have huge red bills. They are usually seen in riverside forests. The Grey Hornbill is smaller again. You see pairs, or small parties, of these hornbills in open woods rather than in true forests. They are greyish-brown birds with black bills.

There is also the huge Ground Hornbill, a most impressive black and white bird the size of a turkey. It has patches of blue and red skin on its face and a great black bill like a pick-axe, which is surmounted by a cylinder-shaped casque open in front. Ground Hornbills live in quite open country, and you often see small parties in the Murchison Falls Park. They stalk about on the ground looking for reptiles and small animals on which they usually feed in preference to fruit. They sometimes eat quite large snakes.

All kinds of hornbill nest in holes in trees, using the same holes year after year. The females of all except the Ground Hornbill are plastered up in their holes with mud. The female, and later the young birds, are fed through a slit which is left open for this purpose. You sometimes read that the mother-bird is being cruelly treated by her mate and forcibly made to attend to her duties. Of course, this is not so. She actually walls herself up with material brought to her by the male, who shows later that he is prepared to work for her and feed her throughout the long breeding period. If the mud wall of the nest gets broken by accident, the female shuts herself in again. An arrangement of this sort, which naturally provides excellent protection against predators, is only possible where food is plentiful and where there is no danger of the bird starving in its cell.

The female Casqued Hornbill stays in her hole for over four months, from before she has laid her eggs until after she has hatched and reared the young birds. She undergoes a complete moult and change of feathers during this confinement, and is so fat and weak when she first emerges that she cannot fly for several days. The Crowned and Grey Hornbills break out of their holes half way through the fledgling period, and then the young birds shut themselves in again. The mother, in her turn, joins her mate and helps him bring food to them. Male and female hornbills appear to become very devoted to one another and probably pair for life. I once heard of a female Casqued Hornbill being stolen by another male before she was completely shut in. For weeks after this her original mate kept on returning to the empty hole, peering into it and groaning as if with anguish.

Female Ground Hornbills are not walled in, probably because of the difficulty of closing up the huge holes they need to nest in. But they sit very tight in their holes and nearly all their food is carried to them by the male and other members of the family or troop. Offerings of food are usually brought at quite regular intervals, two or three times a day, when you see little processions of hornbills flying up to the nest one after the other. Ground Hornbills line the inside of their nesting holes with leaves, and if the female should go away for any reason, as she sometimes does, she is believed to cover the eggs carefully before departing. Ground Hornbills breed irregularly and take several years to grow up.

You usually find Ground Hornbills where there are big trees in the grassland, and they seem to spend almost the whole of their lives hunting and searching for food in the same area. In the Murchison Park, for example, there is a certain group of trees alongside the track which leads to the Albert Nile where you always see Ground Hornbills. They roost in these trees and fly down to the ground as soon as it gets light in the morning. Then you hear their great booming calls which are among the deepest notes produced by any African bird. They feed on the ground in the mornings and again in the evenings, spending the hottest hours of the day resting in the shade either on a perch or on the ground. At feeding time there are usually five or six of these huge hornbills, probably all members of the same family, marching about together looking for food in the grass.

Many Africans seem to regard Ground Hornbills as lazy birds, and the Acholi people have a proverb which they use of someone who is so idle that he is incapable of providing for himself even in times of plenty: *The Ground Hornbill stays hungry when the locusts are swarming.* But I do not know why these birds should be considered as particularly idle.

6

Birds of the Plains and Bushland

Most of the country in the Parks is plain and bushland. This is where the game animals roam and where you are most likely to see lions. Forest covers only a small part of the total area. In some places there are hardly any trees. Elsewhere the land is lightly wooded so that the division between woodland and bushland is not always clear. Trees and shrubs grow in the grassland, and are occupied by birds of several kinds, each using them in a different way.

Grey, stiff-tailed, little Mousebirds, or Colies, creep about looking for fruit and berries, performing all sorts of acrobatic tricks. Scimitar-bills and Green Wood Hoopoes seem to be doing much the same as they probe for insects in cracks and crevices in the bark. In spite of their name, Wood Hoopoes are more akin to Tree Creepers than to true Hoopoes, which are also present in the Parks. Hoopoes roost and nest in trees, but you usually see them on bare ground where they dig for grubs and ants with their sharp bills which look like miniature pick-axes. It is almost impossible to distinguish African Hoopoes from the European Hoopoes which migrate and join them for part of the year. Both kinds have the same black and white wings and fan-like crests, though the African birds are slightly darker.

Rollers perch on isolated trees, often choosing a dead branch as a look-out post. They swoop to catch insects with a curious rolling flight, and travel about the country following the rains. European Rollers, or Blue Jays, are mainly blue and chestnut, and have short square tails. They visit the Parks between October and March. You see Abyssinian Rollers throughout the year, however. They are very similar but have forked tails.

Fiscal Shrikes also swoop for insects from suitable vantage points in the bushland. They eat small birds and animals as well, and have earned for themselves the name of Butcher Birds. At times they establish 'larders', impaling their prey on thorns or on the sharp-pointed leaves of such plants as the wild bow-hemp. Fiscals, which are black and white birds, are the commonest of the many different kinds of shrike which live in the Parks. Like all shrikes they have hooked bills and resemble small hawks in certain respects. The long-tailed glossy black Drongos have some of the same habits. They also swoop from trees as they hunt for insects, performing quite remarkable aerobatics as they do so. Drongos are most pugnacious. A Drongo will attack any bird of any species that dares to enter its territory.

There are a great many ant-hills in the bushland – large mounds of earth constructed by termites, or white ants. White ants develop wings and swarm during the rains, when they are known as 'flying ants'. Many kinds of bird then collect to feed upon them. Birds also follow the bush fires, eating the insects which are disturbed by the flames sweeping through the grass.

Water birds spend most of their time on or near the rivers and lakes, but many also move quite a long way from water for part of the day. Large stretches of water are avoided by some, including certain species of both heron and stork. Black-headed Herons, which are very much like the European Grey Herons, usually forage on dry land though they also fish. The Open-bill Stork, a black bird with a bill that is permanently agape for part of its length, shows a preference for small pools or swampy places in the plains. These storks normally feed on snails, and their peculiar bills are ideal for gripping and crushing the shells. They are particularly partial to a large water-snail which they usually crush under water. You find the Open-bills where these snails are plentiful; these birds seldom stay in the same place for long.

There are also two migrant storks: the White Stork, and Abdim's or the White-bellied Stork. The main nesting ground of the White Storks is in eastern Europe, and they are among the most prominent of the birds which take part in the Autumn migration to Africa. They seldom spend very long in the tropics as, after resting for a day or two in such areas as the Queen Elizabeth Park, they fly straight on to southern Africa. During recent years, many White Storks have taken to breeding in South Africa and spending the whole year there instead or returning to Europe where, today, they are much less common than they used to be. So fewer migrate nowadays, and you do not often see them in the Parks. When you do see them, they often seem to be exhausted by their long flight.

Abdim's Storks are completely black except for their white bellies, which are very obvious in the air. They mostly breed in the Sudan, and migrate southwards with the rains, usually in October or November. They travel in huge untidy flocks, which may number several thousand birds, and only stay for a few days before moving on. They fly as far south as the Transvaal, moving northwards again at the beginning of April when it is raining north of the equator. By this means, Abdim's Storks manage to spend the whole of their lives in wet weather which provides them with abundant food. They eat frogs, small lizards and such insects as grasshoppers. They are particularly partial to locusts and are often called 'Locust Birds' in Africa – White Storks are also given this name in some areas. They do a great deal of good by destroying these pests and are welcomed as a sign of approaching rain.

Pennant-wing Nightjars travel in the opposite direction, and you find them where white ants are swarming. They are one of the seven species of nightjar that appear in the Parks. Nightjars of one kind or another are found almost all over the world. They are generally mottled in colour and are very difficult to see as they rest on the ground in the daytime. They take wing at dusk, and you frequently notice them after dark, especially on moonlight nights. They fly around catching insects in their open mouths, just as swifts and swallows do during the day.

The males of most species of nightjar are much the same as the females. Only a few develop special breeding plumage. But the male Pennant-wing Nightjar grows long white streamers which trail out behind him as he flies; and the male Standard-wing Nightjar grows long shafts to his wings with broad, feathered vanes, or blades, at the tip. These strange ornaments have no function other than courtship display. The birds dance and swoop in the air, vibrating their wings rapidly. The vanes and pennants seem to sail along independently of the birds and look quite ghostly in the moonlight. Like most kinds of nightjar, these have weird, distinctive calls. When you sit by the dying embers of a camp fire in the bush, listening perhaps to the distant roar of a lion or the sawing grunt of a leopard on the prowl, the nightjar's call has an eerie feel about it.

Swifts and swallows fly out from Europe to join the many species of both that live in Africa throughout the year. It is even possible that a few British swifts may find their way to the Parks. No swift ringed in Britain has yet been recovered in Uganda; but they have been found in Rhodesia and Malawi, so some must pass over that country. Swifts spend more time in the air than any other kind of bird, and are exceptionally fast fliers. Most species are capable of seventy or eighty miles an hour, one Asian species being reputed to fly at almost two hundred miles an hour. Both swifts and swallows spend long hours on the wing searching for insects, and are particularly fortunate when the lake-flies swarm. Then you see mixed flocks of swifts, swallows and martins. They swoop and feed, collecting as much as they can in their wide-open mouths.

You see the large Alpine Swifts in the Queen Elizabeth Park. At night they roost in cliffs at an altitude of thirteen thousand feet in the Ruwenzori mountains. Each morning they fly down to the plains, thirty miles away and ten thousand feet below, to feed on the insects that they find there. Palm Swifts behave quite differently. They seem to spend their lives wheeling round the borassus palm trees. They rarely fly far from these trees and nest on them in a most remarkable way. First the swift sticks a pad of feathers to a palm leaf, using its own saliva as a glue. It then fixes its eggs to the feathers and incubates them by clinging to the pad. In their turn, the young swifts also cling to the precarious nest which sways about continuously in the wind.

The Palm Swift is an excellent example of a bird whose life depends entirely on a certain kind of tree. Another example, of a very different sort, is the Palm Nut Vulture, a bird of prey which looks rather like a Fish Eagle. It feeds largely on the nuts produced by palm trees though it does occasionally eat slugs, snails and even small mammals. A few Palm Nut Vultures appear in the Parks when the palms are fruiting in the swamps. You never see them at any other time.

Swallows and martins are very familiar birds in Britain. Swallows build nests with an open top. House Martins build mud nests with a closed top and a small opening. Sand Martins breed in banks. Martins generally have less deeply forked tails than swallows. In Africa, where there are so many more different species, it is less easy to distinguish swallows from martins. Some species of swallow make the same kind of nest as the European Swallow but others, including the Abyssinian Red-rumped Swallow that you find in the Parks, make mud nests with a covered top and a longish entrance tube. African Rock Martins make open saucer-shaped nests like European Swallows. African

A Grey-headed Gull stands beside a Uganda Crested Crane

Wheatear

A Crocodile sleeps below a
tree festooned with the nests of
Black-headed Weavers

Sand Martins dig holes in banks like European Sand Martins. But the White-headed Rough-wing Swallow, which is quite common in the Queen Elizabeth Park, digs a hole in the ground and sometimes even uses holes that are already there.

Where there are flowers there are nearly always sunbirds, or honey-suckers as they are sometimes called. Sunbirds are among the most beautiful birds on earth, and closely resemble the humming-birds of America. They are small and brilliantly coloured, and seem to flash like jewels as they flit from one flower to another in the sunlight. There are many different species, and you find them in every kind of habitat. They hover in front of the flowers and probe for nectar with their long curved bills and long tongues. If a sunbird cannot reach into a large trumpet-shaped flower, it sometimes bores a little hole at the side and gets at the nectar that way. Sunbirds also eat insects. They make pear-shaped nests of grass and leaves, woven together with cobwebs. You see these hanging from branches in the bushland.

Male sunbirds, some of which have magnificent long tails, are almost always more brightly coloured than the females. The male Scarlet-breasted Sunbird, the species you see most often in the Parks, is a brilliant little bird, browny-black with a shining green head and a scarlet breast. The female is a dull brown and buff. Like most kinds of sunbird, they are much attracted by red and yellow flowers and do not scorn garden varieties. A bed of red canna lilies grew beside my office in the Queen Elizabeth Park. As I sat at my desk, the sunbirds used to visit me. They hovered and probed just outside my window, only a foot or two away.

Wherever you look in the bushland you see the nests of small birds. There are places, particularly near swamps and pools, where shrubs and the lower branches of such trees as acacias seem to be festooned with nests. Many of the nests are round. Some hang from branches. Others are attached directly to the trees. Others again are fixed to reeds or grass. Most are about the size of

7

grapefruit, and some trees look as if large fruits are growing on them. If you examine these nests you will find that they are made of grass and fibres beautifully woven together. They are the work of the seed-eaters, the weaver-birds and the buntings.

There are hundreds of different kinds of weaver-bird; fifty have been recorded in the National Parks alone. Their home is the grasslands, the cultivated fields and the villages. They vary in length from about seven inches to just under four inches. They have the short, thick bills of birds which normally eat hard seeds. Many of these little birds are very sparrow-like in appearance.

Weaver-birds are of two main kinds: the true weavers and the smaller weaver-finches. Most of the true weavers have some black and yellow in their plumage, particularly when the males are in breeding condition. They mostly make beautifully woven nests which hang from stems or branches. Weaver-finches do not hang their nests, nor do they make them so carefully.

The commonest true weaver is the Black-headed Weaver. The females are brownish-coloured birds with some yellow on their heads, wings and tails. The males are like this when not in their breeding plumage. When in their breeding plumage, however, they are a glossy black and yellow. You can usually see some in this condition as they breed at almost any time of the year. Their nests, which seem to be everywhere, hang from bushes or the lower branches of acacia trees.

It is marvellous to watch these weavers building their nests. The male does the work and only summons his mate when he is ready for her to finish off the nest with a lining of soft feathers. He uses grass, fibres and strips which he tears off large, stout leaves such as palms – he cuts the leaf with his bill and tears it by flying away with an end in his mouth. When he reaches the tree where he intends to build, he holds one end of the fibre under his foot and the other in his bill. He first twists this end round a small branch. Then he takes the end from under his foot and does the same, so providing himself with a loop in which to stand and work. After doing this, he flies away, collects more fibres and weaves them together, pushing and pulling with his bill and occasionally tying a knot. He makes hundreds of journeys and works away for several days. He first makes a kind of hammock, and this eventually becomes a hanging nest with a short entrance funnel at the bottom. He always works from the inside. Black-headed Weavers nest in colonies, which means that you see several birds working together at the same tree.

Spectacled Weavers, rather shy birds, are similar, but the males keep their black and yellow plumage throughout the year. They make much the same sort of nest adding a somewhat longer entrance funnel. Each pair of these weavers nests in its own tree, and you see the nests hanging from the tip of a convenient bough. Grosbeak Weavers are larger, less brightly coloured and have big clumsy-looking bills. Even so, their nests are more finely woven than those made by any of the other birds in this group. They choose a swampy place, attaching their nests to reeds and building them out of grass. Grosbeak Weavers nest together in small colonies.

Most kinds of weaver-bird spend the whole of their lives near their nesting places. Red-billed Queleas, however, are very restless birds and move about from one part of the country to another looking for the seeds they like. They travel in enormous flocks, which may number millions of birds, and do terrible damage to corn fields. Their numbers build up so greatly because they start breeding exceptionally young, probably when they are no more than six months old. They seem to breed wherever they happen to be when the rains are particularly good, making flimsy nests in the long grass.

You usually see several kinds of weaver-finch together on bare dusty ground. There may be fire-finches, waxbills, bishop-birds, widow-birds and whydahs. Like the sparrows and starlings in

Europe, these small finches have learnt to live with man. They collect around houses and in villages; you find them near the safari lodges as well as out in the bush. Many weaver-finches are brightly coloured. They nest in the grass or in low growing bushes.

I find the Fire-crowned Bishops most attractive. When they are not breeding, their colouring is quite dull. In the breeding season, however, the male becomes a marvellous glossy black and red and is as conspicuous as a little fire-ball. Bishops have a strong sense of territory, and each male has several mates. You see him surrounded by his females with his feathers puffed out so that he looks twice his normal size. He perches on a swaying blade of grass and sings away. Then he rises up into the air and hovers two or three feet above the ground with his wings beating so fast that they hum. Sometimes he claps them together above his back. The female Bishops lay their eggs in small oval nests which are attached to the grass in the male's territory.

Fire-finches, commonly spoken of as Plum Birds, are also brightly coloured. The Red-billed Fire-finch is probably the tamest, and possibly the commonest, bird in East Africa. Wax-bills are plentiful, too. Their plumage is dull but their courtship behaviour is interesting. The male carries bits of grass and straw in his bill and offers them to his mate. Waxbills roost on top of their nests.

Most kinds of widow-bird and whydah are predominantly black, the males of many species developing splendid long tails in the breeding season. The female Paradise Whydah is an inconspicuous little bird about four inches long. The male is the same except during the breeding season. Then he develops an eleven-inch tail which stands out from his rump like a skirt with a bustle. He also develops a fine golden collar and a chestnut-coloured breast. Paradise Whydahs look as if they find difficulty in flying with these tails. They soar in the air and then drop straight down so that their flight is very uneven – they always look to me as if they are 'treading water' in the air. The Pin-tailed Whydah also grows a long tail, but it is less spectacular. Neither of these whydahs makes its own nest. They use the nests of wax-bills and other species when their owners have finished with them.

Canaries, seed-eaters and several different kinds of bunting are also common in the grassland.

Larks, pipits and wagtails behave much as they do in Europe. Indeed, several species are migrants. All these birds spend most of their time on the ground in open country. They nest there and feed there. Many species of lark simply run along the ground when disturbed. Others rise up and sing above their territories, just as the Skylark does in Britain. The Flappet Lark, which is one of the commonest, beats its wings together when in the air, producing a series of loud cracks. No one really knows the purpose of this. It may be part of the Flappet Lark's courtship display, but they seem liable to do it at all seasons.

Yellow Wagtails may be seen almost anywhere in open country. White Wagtails and Grey Wagtails prefer to stay near water. The African Pied Wagtails, which closely resemble the familiar White Wagtails of Britain, always appear to be very friendly birds They often live near houses and, having a strong sense of territory, a pair usually stays in the same locality for years. They fly on to the bonnets of motor cars and agitate around in front of mirrors or bright metal. They may see their own reflections and take this for a rival wagtail, but they may sometimes mistake the glitter of metal for water in which to bathe. Whatever the explanation, it is an attractive habit as there are many places in the Parks where the wagtails seem to be giving you a warm and friendly welcome. As you arrive by launch at the landing stage below the Murchison Falls, two Pied Wagtails invariably come on board to bring you ashore with their greeting.

White-necked Ravens live in the cliffs of the crater hills in the Queen Elizabeth Park. You see them flying over the plains in this region. Pied Crows, which have white collars and white chests, prefer to scavenge around the Park buildings helping to keep these places clean. There are several species of starling. Ruppell's Long-tailed Glossy Starling is one of the finest as well as being one of those most often seen.

African thrushes are not very common. But Sooty Chats, which are members of the same family and are slightly smaller than the Song Thrush, seem to be everywhere in the grassland. The male is black with vividly white patches on its wings and shoulders. The female is a dull brown colour. You see pairs of these little birds flying from one ant-hill to the next. They nest in these ant-hills and feed largely on ants and termites. Their lives revolve round ants to such an extent that they are often called Anteater Chats.

Common Wheatears are migrants which I particularly liked to see in the grasslands of Africa. In Cornwall, where I live in England, I enjoy watching them on the downs behind my house, as large numbers congregate there in the autumn before leaving for their winter quarters in Africa. They flit around and dart after insects, their white rumps flashing in the sunlight.

In some ways the most typical inhabitants of the plains and bushland are the game birds. This rather vague expression refers to the guinea-fowl, francolins, spurfowl, quails and bustards. The first four belong to the same family as the pheasants and partridges. Bustards share many of their habits and look rather like enormous partridges with long necks and long legs. All these birds are good to eat though, of course, no shooting is allowed in National Parks.

Game-birds feed on the ground and nest on the ground, making very simple nests or just scraping out little hollows for their eggs. Most of these birds fly well but tend either to run from danger or to sit very tight; then they are difficult to see owing to their grey and brown mottled plumage. They enjoy dust-baths, however, so you often see them on bare open patches or beside the dusty tracks. They have strong legs and blunt claws with which they scratch the ground.

You often see flocks of Tufted Guinea-fowl, which are practically the same as the familiar farmyard birds, busily pecking about on the ground or flying noisily up into the trees where they roost at night. Guinea-fowl are preyed upon by leopards, and where guinea-fowl are plentiful, you usually also find leopards. But guinea-fowl also have many other enemies, such as rats and other small mammals that take the eggs and young chicks. These small predators, in their turn, are also attacked by leopards. In this way leopards actually help to maintain the numbers of guinea-fowl. Leopards protect the very birds upon which they prey, as more of these birds reach maturity where leopards are about.

When ready to breed, the female guinea-fowl stands in front of the male, who shakes his tail, stamps his feet and spins round, dragging one wing on the ground. The female does not make a proper nest but simply scrapes out a hole for her eggs. The chicks can walk almost immediately after hatching and, at night, creep up into low-growing bushes long before they are able to fly up into their roosting trees. As well as the Tufted Guinea-fowl there is a rare and beautiful Crested Guinea-fowl living in the forests.

The only difference between francolins and spurfowl is that spurfowl have patches of bare skin on their throats. Both look very much like partridges but usually have some bright red or yellow colouring on their heads, necks and wings. There are numerous species of both francolin and spurfowl, and several of them are plentiful in different parts of the Parks. Some stay by themselves. Others live together in coveys like partridges. Most have the habit of hiding in small patches of bush, but some may often be seen standing on ant-hills.

Quails are much smaller than francolins or guinea-fowl and travel much further, although their movements and migrations are extremely difficult to understand. European Quails fly out to Africa. Cape Quails, from South Africa, fly north as far as Sudan to avoid the southern winter. They are almost identical so that it is difficult to tell which kind you are looking at. Harlequin Quails, lovely little birds coloured black and white and chestnut, move about Africa from east to west as well as from north to south. They appear to follow the rains but, even so, have no definite seasons for their migrations and no fixed breeding territories. Their arrival in the Parks is quite unpredictable. They sometimes travel in very large flocks.

Many years ago I was attending a high level security meeting in Kampala. A bird flew in at the window and settled on the safe in which all the secret documents were kept. The Governor and the Commissioner of Police seemed safely engaged on affairs of state, and only one other person, a kindred spirit, seemed to have noticed the new arrival. I caught his eye, crept out of my seat, seized the waste-paper basket and popped it over the little bird before anyone else realized what was happening. It was a Harlequin Quail exhausted by its long flight. After a day of rest and food it resumed its journey.

Bustards make a complete contrast to these little birds. The Black-bellied Bustard stands about two feet and is a familiar sight in the grassland. Although you usually see them walking or running, they are fast, powerful fliers and look rather like dark swans in the air. The male has an usual display flight: he flies up to a great height above his territory and then planes steeply down without moving his wings which he holds well up above his back. The female makes no nest but simply lays her eggs on the ground.

The only other kind of bustard seen in the Parks is Jackson's Bustard, an enormous bird which stands three feet tall and has a thick, tawny neck-mane. You only see them in the Murchison Park where they stalk about in the grassland holding their heads up in a most stately way. Jackson's Bustards do not live in the Park throughout the year. They arrive in February, when the grass fires are over, and stay for several months during which they breed. When displaying the male seems to turn himself almost inside out. He erects the feathers of his neck until they form a great white ruff which completely covers his head. The bird then looks like an enormous white ball rolling about on the plains.

Jackson's Bustards favour particularly the scattered bush country near the Albert Nile where there are always large herds of antelopes. The very beautiful Carmine Bee-eater, which is carmine-red and green in colour and has a long tail, arrives in the area at about the same time. Like other bee-eaters, these perch and swoop for insects, sometimes using the back of an antelope as a perch. They also accompany the Jackson's Bustards. If you are very lucky you may see a Carmine Bee-eater riding jockey-fashion on the back of one of these huge birds.

Bustards are actually more closely related to cranes than to the other game-birds. Cranes are splendid birds, the Crested Cranes of Africa being probably the most colourful of all the many different kinds. The Uganda Crested Crane stands over three feet on slender black legs. Its plumage is generally white, maroon, black and grey; its face is black, enamel-white and crimson; there are vivid scarlet wattles at its throat, and its head is topped by an upright tuft of stiff amber-coloured bristles.

These glorious-looking birds stalk about the grassland searching for insect food. You see them in the short grass country near the Albert Nile and on the Ishasha plains in the Queen Elizabeth Park where buffaloes are their companions. You frequently hear the long-drawn-out, two-syllabled trumpeting call which Crested Cranes make as they fly overhead in formation. It is a strangely beautiful sound, very typical of this part of Africa. All kinds of crane have striking calls, made possible by the peculiar construction of their wind-pipes.

Crested Cranes excel at dancing. They pirouette, bob and bow to one another in a solemn, stately way, holding their wings wide open and high above their backs. Sometimes mixed parties dance together. At other times, the males dance while the females look on. These dancing displays do not only take place during courtship. You may see them at any time. During the breeding season, the male Crested Crane also performs another ceremony. He stands, stooped and hunched up, with his head back and one wing raised. In this strange posture, he points his bill towards the sky and utters his deep, booming mating call which is not heard very often. Crested Cranes nest in meadows and roost in trees, showing a particular liking for flat-topped acacias.

In some respects, cranes resemble both storks and herons, which have been described in some detail in earlier chapters, although there are several obvious differences. Storks are almost silent. Herons are not silent but have no calls that can be compared with the musical notes produced by cranes. Neither storks nor herons fly in formation as cranes do. Herons fly with their necks doubled back on their shoulders. Cranes fly rather like storks with their necks stretched forward but in a slightly downward curve. The Crested Crane is one of Africa's most fascinating birds. It is the national emblem of Uganda.

7

Birds of Prey

Birds of prey, probably the most thrilling of all birds, are seldom seen in Britain nowadays. Buzzards, kestrels and sparrowhawks are still fairly common in some regions, but anything else is quite a rare sight except in parts of Scotland. In Africa, by contrast, there are large numbers of these birds, among them more big eagles than anywhere else in the world. During a few hours spent in the National Parks you may expect to see fifteen or twenty different species of hawk and eagle as well as flocks of vultures.

The Secretary Bird is the most unusual of them, and you often see a pair in the short grass country near the Albert Nile. Secretary Birds stand over three feet tall on long, slender legs so that, from a distance, they look like storks or herons. But the shape of their heads, and their powerful hooked bills, show clearly that they are birds of prey. They are generally grey in colour with a good deal of black on their wings and tails. There are also several long black feathers sticking out like plumes from the back of the Secretary Bird's head. These feathers are erected when the bird is angry, or surprised, making it look like an old-fashioned lawyer's clerk with several quill pens behind his ear. This is not all. The Secretary Bird has a longish tail and black feathers on its thighs which together suggest that it is wearing breeches and a tail coat. There are very good reasons for its name.

You usually see Secretary Birds marching about in the grass-land with slow, deliberate strides. They can fly extremely well, however, and look particularly graceful when taking off or landing. The Secretary Bird runs into the wind holding its wings open to catch the air. Then it soars to a height of several hundred feet, planing downwards and running along the ground as soon as its feet touch down. These birds roost and nest on flat-topped acacia trees, using the same tree for several years. The male is slightly larger than the female, and they are said to pair for life.

Unlike other birds of prey, Secretary Birds always hunt on the ground. They eat small mammals, young birds, insects and reptiles, and they are famous as killers of snakes. They kill by hammering their victims with their exceptionally hard feet. They kill snakes in this way, protecting themselves from the attack of poisonous snakes by using their wings as shields. You sometimes see a pair of Secretary Birds together. More often, when hunting, the two birds stay some distance apart, calling to one another to keep in contact.

Predatory birds, in general, may be divided into three main types: vultures, which are scavengers and carrion-feeders and do not do their own hunting; hawks and eagles, which hunt during the day, killing live animals for food; and owls, which also kill live animals but hunt at night and rest during the day. All these birds have powerful, hooked bills whose function is tearing flesh. Those which kill live prey also have powerful, hooked talons which are their killing weapons. More than fifty species of these birds (vultures, hawks, eagles, owls and their immediate relatives) have been recorded in the National Parks. They differ widely in size, habits and appearance, largely according to the kind of prey they take, their methods of hunting and the sort of country they inhabit.

Vultures are generally thought of as objectionable or even disgusting birds. Certainly, their feeding habits are not very pleasant. Nor can their appearance be described as attractive, particularly when you see them on the ground, or perched on a tree, waiting for a lion to abandon its kill or, worse, for a sick animal to die. They have ugly, bare heads and faces, a sign of their feeding habits, as feathers on their heads would get into a frightful mess from the rotting flesh they often eat. The vultures sit in a hunched-up position and sometimes draw their heads right down into the ruff of feathers round their necks. They usually nest at the top of a tall tree, sometimes on a rocky ledge.

In the air, however, vultures are magnificent birds. They soar for hours on their huge wings, waiting and watching everything that is happening on the ground. They have exceptionally good eye-sight and sometimes fly so high that they are invisible to the naked human eye. Yet they themselves see where the lions are hunting. They notice sick or young animals that have been abandoned by the herds. They see the gangs of poachers at work in outlying parts of the Park, and circle overhead ready to descend as soon as carrion becomes available.

For these reasons, the Warden finds that vultures are the most useful of all birds. He watches them circling in the sky. If they show any sign of descending to the ground, he goes there immediately and almost always discovers something interesting. By this means the Warden can tell where the lions are hunting, or if there has been an outbreak of disease among any of the herds of animals under his charge. The Warden also learns the whereabouts of poachers as vultures show the position of a carcase or a camp. Finding and arresting poachers is one of his most difficult tasks. If there were no vultures to show the way, very few would ever be caught.

Vultures also keep the country clean. They only scavenge where it is fairly open, however. In the forests, trees and dense foliage make it impossible for soaring birds to see the ground; there the carrion is eaten by insects and those mammals that take such food.

There are several different kinds of vulture. The commonest is

the White-backed Vulture, a buff-coloured bird with a dark face
and bill, and a seven-foot wing-span. The largest is the Lappet-
faced Vulture which is darker and has a nine-foot wing-span. The
smallest of those likely to be seen in the National Parks is the
Hooded Vulture which has a bare pink face and a pink bill. There
are others, but from a distance they all look much the same except
for their size.

If you can get to a carcase before the vultures, it is fascinating
to sit and watch from a short distance away. Ten or twelve
Hooded Vultures usually arrive first. They settle on a nearby tree,
or on the ground, and approach cautiously like guests who are
uncertain of their welcome. If the carcase is that of a large animal
they start feeding as far away from the head as they can, probably
to make sure that it is really dead. The White-backed Vultures
follow, in much greater numbers, so that the Hooded Vultures are
soon pushed out of the way. The carcase becomes a heaving,
scrambling mass of White-backed Vultures tearing at the meat
and fighting greedily for whatever they can get. The Hooded
Vultures retire, wait on the outskirts and dash in for an occasional
morsel.

The larger species do not come immediately. Lappet-faced
Vultures hardly ever appear until the others have been feeding for
about half an hour. Then one or two of these great birds arrive,
and the White-backed Vultures make way for them. Last on the
scene is the White-headed Vulture, usually only a single bird.
This vulture is no larger than the White-backed but has a powerful red bill and is altogether more eagle-like. It settles on the
ground and then walks purposefully into the seething mass of
inferior birds, taking its time and feeding slowly.

When fully gorged, and there is nothing more for them to eat,
the vultures retire to nearby trees to digest their meal. Some stay
on the ground, holding their wings half-open as cormorants do
when they have finished fishing; they probably find that this helps

their digestions. The late arrivals are the first to leave. The Hooded Vultures stay longest. They hope, no doubt, that something may be left after the larger birds have finished.

The true birds of prey are the various falcons, hawks and eagles which hunt for live prey during the hours of daylight. They vary in size from the Little Sparrowhawk, which is not much larger than a thrush, to great eagles whose opened wings span seven feet. They are divided into several distinct groups nearly all of which are represented in the Parks. They are found in every type of habitat, though the majority hunt in open country.

Falcons, such as the Peregrine and Kestrel, have long, pointed wings, and are exceptionally fast, powerful fliers. Most species are between twelve and eighteen inches long. Many of them kill other birds in the air by striking them with their hind claws when flying at top speed. Kestrels do not do this. They hover and drop to kill their prey on the ground.

Sparrowhawks and Goshawks have short rounded wings and long tails. They hunt in forest or woodland, flying low down between the trees. They show great agility in flight as they chase their prey in these conditions, sometimes seizing a bird in the air, at others pouncing on some small creature on the ground. You often see the grey Chanting Goshawk perched on a branch, waiting patiently for the chance to strike.

Harriers are long-tailed and long-winged hawks which fly low over open country, killing their prey on the ground. Montagu's Harriers, Marsh Harriers and Pallid Harriers, all of which are migrants from Europe, may be seen in the Parks between October and March. In Britain, the sight of any of these birds is a comparatively rare and exciting event. In the Queen Elizabeth Park I used sometimes to watch the Montagu's Harriers from the verandah of my house as they quartered the flat ground alongside Lake Edward. The male is a beautiful pale grey bird. The female is coloured brown. Harriers hold their prey with one foot when flying, and you may sometimes see the male pass this across to the female in the air, though this rarely happens away from the nesting area.

There are several different kinds of buzzard. They have short, square tails and broad wings. Kites, by contrast, have long wings and forked tails. Their feet and claws are comparatively weak; though they are able to kill small birds and animals, they feed mainly on carrion and the larger insects. Tropical African Kites are very numerous and often make a nuisance of themselves by raiding chicken-runs and searching for scraps.

The true eagles are the most magnificent of all birds of prey. Their legs and feet are covered with feathers down to the base of their toes, a characteristic which distinguishes these eagles from hawks and such birds as the Harrier Eagle. Most eagles have a majestic, soaring flight and generally hunt by pouncing on their prey. The eagle flies down with half-closed wings and claws spread out. It seizes its prey and holds it to the ground, giving a mighty clutch with its talons. The attack is so violent that the victim is usually killed immediately. The eagle may then feed, or it may fly away with its prey held firmly in its claws. The attack is not always fatal, however; I have heard of a mongoose scurrying away, apparently undamaged, after being dropped by an eagle which was carrying it off.

The Martial Eagle is the largest and finest of the several kinds of eagle that live in the Parks. It is a grey-brown eagle with boldly spotted white underparts and a small but distinct crest on its head. It measures three feet from head to tail, and has a wing-span of seven feet. Its talons are the size of a human hand. The females are larger, darker and more heavily spotted than the males. Martials live in open country, feeding on game birds and small animals up to the size of the smaller antelopes. You sometimes see them in the air but, quite often, a Martial sits proudly on a branch watching and waiting for possible prey. Then you

Black-headed Heron

Pied Kingfisher perching

Lesser Flamingoes feeding in shallow water

Brown Harrier Eagle with young in nest
A female Martial Eagle and her eaglet

may be able to approach one of the world's most exciting birds,
one that is even larger and stronger than the Golden Eagle. The
Martial seems so confident of its own strength that it does not
bother to fly away.

One day I noticed vultures settling and, as usual, went to investigate. When I reached the spot, I saw a half-circle of fifty
or sixty vultures on the ground. They were watching a Martial
feeding on a hare, hoping no doubt for any pickings that the eagle
might leave. The Martial stood with its wings half-open, as
eagles tend to do when tearing at their food. It had its back to the
vultures. If any of them dared to move in closer than the ten yards
or so that separated them, the Martial looked up and turned its
head. That was quite enough to make the vultures keep their
distance.

The Crowned Eagle is another magnificent bird, almost as
large as the Martial and even more powerful. Crowned Eagles are
forest birds. They rarely come out into the open and are seldom
seen. But there are Crowned Eagles in the Maramagambo forest,
and you sometimes see a pair in that part of the Queen Elizabeth
Park. Their colour is almost black and they have shorter wings
and a longer tail than those eagles which hunt over the open plains.
Like huge sparrowhawks, they are able to fly swiftly between the
trees and change direction rapidly.

Crowned Eagles live chiefly on medium-sized forest animals
such as young duikers. They also devote a great deal of time and
energy to hunting monkeys. But monkeys are too agile and their
eye-sight is too good for them to be taken very often. Crowned
Eagles are reputed to use mimicry when hunting monkeys. The
male hides in the foliage of an evergreen forest tree and gives a
soft, whistling call. Hearing this, an adult monkey comes to
investigate and tries to drive the eagle away. This gives the
female eagle the chance to slip in and steal a young member of
the monkey troop. This all seems rather far-fetched, but it is

certainly true that an eagle's best chance of killing a monkey is to seek out a youngster when the adults are interested in something else.

The eagles most often seen over the plains are Wahlberg's Eagles, small brown eagles which look like over-sized kites with square tails. Though these eagles eat almost any small animal at times, they feed chiefly on field rats, grass mice and gerbils, little jumping animals that remind you of miniature kangaroos. Tawny Eagles are somewhat larger. They have a great reputation for ferocity sometimes driving other eagles away from their prey and occasionally robbing other birds in the air. Tawny Eagles do not seem to have any very marked food preferences and habitually eat carrion.

African Hawk Eagles frequent tall trees in the bushland, particularly those which grow along the banks of rivers. African Hawk Eagles do not soar. They fly fast and low, feeding chiefly on birds which they surprise in the open. Sometimes they behave like falcons, taking birds on the wing, and are the great enemies of herons which they attack in this way. These eagles look rather like a smaller edition of the Martial but have longer tails.

The Long-crested Hawk Eagle also favours forest strips. It is a smaller bird, and you often see one perching on a leafless branch with its crest waving in the wind. The Long-crested Hawk Eagle hunts from such a perch. It takes more small lizards than anything else though it also eats rats, mice and even insects. The name 'hawk eagle' is rather confusing. It is used for these birds because of their methods of hunting. They 'hawk' for their prey either by skimming about, or by waiting patiently and then flying straight at whatever it is they are trying to capture. Hawk eagles do not soar. However, they are true eagles with legs feathered down to the toes.

Harrier Eagles or Snake Eagles, on the other hand, have no feathers on their feet. They look rather like large buzzards but have short, rough toes of great strength which enable them to clutch and hold their slippery prey. They feed almost entirely on lizards and snakes, which they swallow whole after first crushing the head. Eagles are not immune to the effects of snake-bite and are occasionally killed by poisonous snakes. They defend themselves with their wings, as do Secretary Birds, but their best defence is their own great agility. It is reckoned that a single Harrier Eagle may kill as many as a hundred snakes in a year; in this respect, these birds are of great benefit to man.

You see several species of Harrier Eagle in the Parks though, from a distance, they are not always easy to distinguish. One, the Short-toed Harrier Eagle, is a migrant from southern Europe. The others live in Africa throughout the year. The commonest of these is the Brown Harrier Eagle which is usually seen in rather lightly wooded country not far from the lakes. It feeds chiefly on tree-snakes, which it seizes when the snake is climbing the trunk of a tree. You sometimes see Short-toed Harrier Eagles hovering like huge kestrels. I once watched one in Spain. It hovered about two hundred feet above the ground, turned down its head and moved into a high speed vertical dive, pulling up twice before dropping into a field of corn.

Two eagles which do not quite fit into either category are the Fish Eagle and the Bateleur. I have described the Fish Eagle already. The Bateleur is a medium-sized eagle with exceptionally long, pointed wings, a very short tail and brilliant colouring: black, chestnut and white with a bare red face and red legs. You frequently see Bateleurs in the Parks, flying at a steady speed of forty or fifty miles an hour about two hundred feet above the ground. They spend most of the day in the air, flying to and fro above their territories. You see them dive to take food from other birds of prey, or to attack some creature on the ground; and they dive menacingly at anyone who goes too near their nests.

Bateleurs are very partial to snakes, and do not hesitate to tackle such dangerous snakes as puff-adders, which they probably attack as often as do any of the Harrier Eagles. They also eat carrion at times, and the absence of feathers on their faces is probably connected with this. But Bateleurs are among the most magnificent of birds. There is nothing of the vulture's meanness in the proud carriage of their heads.

Most kinds of eagle nest in tall trees. The different species often nest quite close together, though two eagles of the same species always nest at a good distance from one another, each in its own hunting territory. You find the nests of Wahlberg's Eagles scattered about in the bushland of the Queen Elizabeth Park, each nest four or five miles from the next. There may be a Martial's nest, a Hawk Eagle's nest and a Bateleur's nest quite close to one of the Wahlberg's. The nearest Martial's nest, however, will be ten or twelve miles away. The explanation of this is that the different kinds of eagle do not compete for the same food. Martial Eagles do not eat the grass-mice favoured by Wahlberg's, the snakes eaten by the Bateleur or the small birds captured by the African Hawk Eagle. The Martial has no reason to object to the presence of these other eagles in its hunting territory. The hunting territories of the different species habitually overlap. Eagles and most other birds of prey have very definite food preferences and only change in times of shortage.

It may seem surprising that so many hawks and eagles should be able to find enough to eat. There are so many small creatures, however, that there is always enough to go round, and these birds kill only a small proportion of their total number. A large eagle eats the equivalent of about one-tenth of its own weight each day. A small hawk may eat a quarter of its own weight. This means that a pair of Martials, weighing about ten pounds each, need only two pounds of food daily. They can kill animals of up to ten pounds but certainly do not do so every day. A Wahlberg's Eagle only eats one small mouse each day: there are thousands of mice in the grasslands of Africa. Eagles are assisted in their hunting by wonderful eye-sight, four times as powerful as man's. A Martial will change direction when in full flight if it sees a flock of guinea-fowl on the ground two miles away.

Eagles sometimes feed on the ground where they have killed. They sometimes carry their prey back to their roosts or nests and, of course, always do so when there are young birds to feed – you often see the bones and skulls of their victims on the ground below a nest. No eagle, however, is able to carry a weight which is as heavy as itself. No eagle is strong enough to fly away carrying a human baby as you are often told. Eagles hardly ever attack man under any circumstances.

A pair of eagles generally uses the same nest for several years, and they sometimes have a second nest which they occupy occasionally. The pair stays together until one or other of the eagles dies. Then the survivor immediately takes a new partner and continues breeding on the same site. In practice, this means a change of mate every five or six years. A Crowned Eagle has lived in a zoo for forty-four years, but it is unlikely that wild eagles live for more than half this time.

Eagles do not breed every year. Martials, and other large eagles, probably breed every other year. The smaller species do so more frequently. Most kinds of eagle lay one or two eggs in a large untidy nest which is made of sticks and lined with grass or leaves. Incubation takes at least six weeks, and the eaglet that emerges is a weak little creature covered with soft down. For some weeks the parents show great tenderness towards it. The male hunts, while the female stays on guard at the nest. He passes his prey to her; she tears it up and feeds small pieces to the eaglet. At six weeks, the eaglet is able to walk about but not to fly. It can tear up its own food by this time, so the older birds merely bring along what they have caught and leave it in the nest. They themselves often use the second nest at this stage in the upbringing of the family. If there are two eaglets together in a nest, they may fight, the stronger killing and eating the weaker.

Depending on the species, young eagles are able to fly between two and four months after hatching. But they cannot kill their own prey and support themselves until they are half grown – this means about ten months old with the larger eagles. So eagles depend on their parents for much longer than most birds. Many die before they are sufficiently mature to breed. Crowned and Martial Eagles do not start breeding until they are at least four years old, though they may pair earlier than this. Wahlberg's, and other small eagles, start breeding when they are about three years old. The courtship activities of most birds of prey take place in the air, when you sometimes see aerobatic displays to rival the Farnborough Air Show.

Owls have the same hooked bills as hawks and eagles; they have the same powerful feet, armed with long talons, which they use for grasping their prey. They also hunt and kill the same kinds of animal, and they occupy much the same place in nature. But owls hunt at night, so that there is no real competition between these two very similar kinds of predatory bird. For example, a Martial Eagle and the huge Verreaux's Eagle Owl are able to hunt over the same territory without interfering with each other. Similarly, the little Pearl-spotted Owlet, which lives in thickish bush and woodland, may be compared with a Sparrowhawk.

The chief difference between owls and other birds of prey is in the senses they employ to detect their victims. Hawks and eagles have exceptionally good eye-sight, as we have seen. So far as is known, they make very little use of their sense of hearing though harriers, whose ears are rather large, may do so when hunting over long grass. Birds generally do not have a very highly developed sense of smell.

Owls lack the wonderfully sharp sight enjoyed by eagles. Even so, they see quite well in daylight and extremely well in poor light when their eyes are ten times as sensitive as human eyes. Much more important, however, is their marvellous power of hearing which, with some species, is assisted by a fringe of feathers on their faces acting as a sound reflector.

Owls fly quite silently and hunt by stealth in almost complete darkness. They hear every sound and movement made by their intended victims which can neither hear nor see them coming. But owls are only able to locate moving prey, so they never feed on carrion or anything else that does not move.

Owls also differ from other predatory birds in their methods of feeding. They do not normally remove the fur or pluck the feathers of their victims. They swallow them whole, or in large chunks, after carrying them away to their perch or nest. Fur, feathers and bones, which cannot be digested, are soon brought up again as pellets formed in the owl's stomach. Most kinds of owl spend the day in hollow trees or in dark places where the foliage is thick. You find these pellets on the ground nearby and, if you examine them carefully, you can see what the owl has been eating.

There are many different kinds of owl, and it is almost certain that some of those living in the Parks have not yet been recorded. You see African Barn Owls quite often as, like their European namesakes, they frequent the neighbourhood of buildings. You sometimes see African Marsh Owls on meadows beside the Nile. Unlike most other kinds of owl, which have rather solitary habits, Marsh Owls tend to collect in small parties and sometimes hunt during the day. They nest on the ground among reeds and rushes, not in trees like most other species. The rare Fishing Owl also appears on the Nile. Fishing owls are very large owls, whose colouring is a rich tawny brown. They inhabit patches of thick forest beside the river and come out in the evening to hunt for fish, when you see them flying low over the water close to the banks.

But the most exciting of all the owls living in the National Parks is Verreaux's Eagle Owl, which has long tufts of feathers growing above its ears and is one of the largest owls in the world. These Eagle Owls are as big as medium-sized eagles but do not have quite the same formidable talons. They kill moderately large animals at times, but are particularly partial to hedgehogs, which they frequently devour after stripping off the spiny part of the skin. The great owl floats down and seizes the hedgehog before it has time to roll itself up into a ball.

Verreaux's Eagle Owls seem to need less shade than most other kinds of owl. They generally use old nests vacated by eagles or vultures, and like to spend the day perched on a tree not far away from their nests. You often see one at the edge of a small patch of woodland near the Albert Nile. When one of these Eagle Owls flies during the day, it is invariably mobbed by any hawks or eagles that catch sight of it. Buzzards, in particular, seem to dislike them intensely. Buzzards are occasionally attacked by these owls at night. In return, they sometimes raid an Eagle Owl's nest during the day.

The small birds and animals of the African bush live in danger of attack from the air at night as well as during the day. They are not safe in any kind of country, though fewer predatory birds hunt in dense forest than in the open bushland. There are so many of these small creatures, however, that their total numbers do not seem to suffer. Birds of prey, moreover, often strike down sick or injured animals which are unable to escape or defend themselves. Most of these would not have much longer to live anyway.

8

Partners and Surroundings of the Birds

An inconspicuous starling-sized bird, known as the Black-throated Honey-guide, lives in the forests and more thickly wooded parts of the Parks. It feeds on grubs and insects, and on the honey and beeswax produced by wild bees – honey-guides are the only birds known to digest and eat wax. In Africa, bees usually swarm in hollow trees or in holes left by such birds as woodpeckers when they have finished nesting. Some of the holes used by bees have very narrow openings, so that the honey-guides, whose bills are small and weak, are unable to dig out the honey without help. They get help either from man, or from an animal known as the ratel or honey-badger.

The ratel is not unlike the European badger, to which it is related, and has exceptionally sharp claws. It climbs well and has a thick, tough skin so is not hurt when bees try to sting it. It is also extremely partial to a meal of honey. Africans eat this wild honey, too. It is much sweeter and tastier than anything you can buy in a shop.

When the honey-guide wants a meal, it looks out for one or other of these helpers. It makes itself as conspicuous as possible by fanning out its tail, hopping about on a bough and calling persistently with a rattling, churring note. After attracting attention to itself in this way, it then flutters on from branch to branch, keeping eight or ten yards ahead of you, until it has reached the bees' nest; it may guide you for half a mile or even more. The bird waits excitedly while the honey is being dug out and as bees often nest high up in tall forest trees, this may take quite a long time.

You should always reward a honey-guide which has led you to a bees' nest by leaving sufficient grubs and wax for it to eat. Africans invariably do this; the bird and the ratel usually feed together. It is said that if you fail to reward the bird, or fail to dig out the honey it has shown you, it will next guide you to a dangerous animal such as a leopard or a poisonous snake. It is also said that the bird will attempt to do this if, for any reason, you fail to follow it when it tries to guide you. Of course, this cannot be true as the bird's guiding habit is instinctive and is not the result of a prepared plan. But there may well be a dangerous animal lying somewhere on the route, along which the honey-guide is leading you, so it is always advisable to go carefully.

I have often followed honey-guides, and enjoyed the honey they have shown me without getting into trouble. But, one evening, a Warden followed a honey-guide which he had ignored earlier in the day when it had tried to persuade him to leave his camp in the bush. He had not gone far before finding that he was walking straight towards a lioness with two young cubs.

The guiding habit must have started as an arrangement between these birds and ratels long before man first appeared on earth. But man, with his tools, is an even more efficient honey-gatherer than the ratel. From the days when human beings first started to roam these forests, honey-guides have made use of them. The arrangement is mutual, however. Africans, on the look-out for honey in the bush, watch for the bird rather than the bee.

There are several kinds of honey-guide though only the Black-throated Honey-guide and one other species, not found in the Parks, show this guiding behaviour. They are rather solitary birds and you nearly always see one by itself. They do not make their own nests but, like cuckoos, lay their eggs in nests taken over from barbets or other forest birds.

The relationship between the honey-guide and the ratel is an outstanding example of *symbiosis* with two completely different kinds of animal being of direct benefit to one another – the bird shows the ratel where to find the honey; the ratel digs it out, and they both share the spoil. We have seen already (in Chapter 3) how Water Thicknees and crocodiles have similarly formed a kind of partnership, and the way in which Carmine Bee-eaters make use of antelopes, and such large birds as Jackson's Bustard, when they are searching for insects. These particular partnerships are one-sided, however, as only the bee-eater gets any obvious advantage from it.

In fact, you seldom see any of the larger mammals without their attendant birds. Most commonly these are Cattle Egrets, or Buff-backed Herons, small white herons whose backs are faintly tinged with buff. These egrets, as they are invariably called, follow the herds of game and feed on the grasshoppers and other insects kicked up by their feet. You can see them walking about among the buffaloes and antelopes when these are feeding. And you seldom see an elephant without at least one attendant egret.

The dazzling white plumage of the Cattle Egret shows up strikingly against the dark mass of an elephant. Sometimes the bird stands beside the elephant looking rather pompous as if it is proud of having such an important friend. Sometimes it rides on the elephant's back or head. The egrets do not do this to feed on ticks, or on any of the other parasites to be found on an elephant's skin, but to take advantage of a moving perch. The bird flies too fast, but walks too slowly, for an elephant on the move. The only way it can keep pace is by riding.

Piapiacs also behave like this. They are small, noisy members of the crow family, and are very common in the Murchison Falls

Park. They are dark, glossy birds which are not much larger than starlings but have long, wedge-shaped tails like magpies. Piapiacs are extremely noisy, and you generally see little parties together giving the impression that they are quarrelling violently among themselves. For this reason they are sometimes spoken of as 'The Seven Sisters'.

Both Cattle Egrets and Piapiacs have the same purpose: to feed on insects disturbed by the elephant's feet. Both sometimes resort to strange tricks to make an elephant move through the grass. You see them deliberately annoying an elephant to make it charge. Occasionally whole flocks of these birds fly round a single elephant in the open, or they may walk slowly towards one in a menacing way. Egrets sometimes fly round herds of elephants and actually drive them away from a feeding ground so that they themselves can feast on the insects disturbed by the fleeing herd.

Ox-peckers make an even closer partnership with the larger mammals. They are pale brown birds of the same family as starlings and are of two kinds: Yellow-billed Ox-peckers, which occur in the Parks, and the Red-billed Ox-peckers which are common further east. They climb about the bodies of large animals, such as buffaloes, rhinoceroses and giraffes, searching for ticks and other external parasites. When doing this they look rather like woodpeckers, particularly if you see them clambering about the neck of a giraffe as if it were the trunk of a tree.

Ox-peckers search the bodies of their animal hosts with great care. They peck away at such sensitive places as the eyes, ears and nostrils. They peck at open sores, and sometimes even eat the flesh, when their attentions must be most painful. Elephants will not have anything to do with them. If an ox-pecker settles on an elephant, it is picked off immediately and removed by the animal's trunk. In general, however, the arrangement benefits the hosts. The birds help to rid them of ticks and other equally troublesome pests. They also act as sentinels, warning an animal when a hunter, or other danger, is approaching. At times the warning works the wrong way round.

One day I was walking across open, treeless country in the Murchison Falls Park, talking to one of our Rangers about a new track we were planning. There did not seem to be any animals about, and neither of us was taking particular care. We wanted a good vantage point, saw what we thought was a small ant-hill some distance ahead and walked towards it. When we were about thirty yards off, an ox-pecker got up excitedly. We turned and tip-toed quietly away. We had not been walking towards an ant-hill. The bird had saved us from trying to use a sleeping rhinoceros as a foot-stool.

This is not the end of the ox-pecker's relationship with these various mammals. Ox-peckers nest in a convenient hole in a tree. They line their nests with hair collected from the animals on which they ride and feed.

You sometimes see birds of other kinds riding on the backs of the larger animals, and some of them are undoubtedly looking for ticks or insects. We have seen already how wagtails and sandpipers search the scales of crocodiles. Ravens, crows and starlings occasionally settle on the backs of buffaloes or antelopes, probably for the same reason. You see Hammerheads, Egyptian Geese and other birds on the backs of hippopotamuses in the water. Almost certainly, however, their concern is only to make use of a convenient perch. But all these are very temporary associations; they are in no way the same as the permanent partnerships entered into by some of the other species. Yellow-billed Ox-peckers and Cattle Egrets, in particular, are hardly ever seen where there are no large mammals.

In this book I have written about less than half the total number of bird species known to live in, or visit, the Uganda National Parks. However, I have mentioned at least one member of each of the sixty-five families represented in the area, and I have described most of the more interesting and more numerous species.

We have seen all these birds against the background of their surroundings; not only the country and the vegetation but also the various animals that share these with them. We have seen how the birds depend on these surroundings, not only for their food but in many other matters such as nesting and roosting. We have seen how the shape and colouring of the birds' bodies (legs, feet, wings, bills and so on) vary with the kind of country they inhabit. This is the *ecological* picture of the birds in the Uganda National Parks: their relationship to the other animals and the plants among which they live.

We have seen how certain kinds of bird favour certain habitats, and we have looked at the reasons for this. But the whole of an apparently suitable habitat is not equally used, a fact which is not at all easy to explain. Why should the Ground Hornbills in the Murchison Falls Park favour one group of trees and not another? Why should Jackson's Bustards stay on the grassland near the Albert Nile and never visit another part of the Park which seems to us to be just as suitable?

This may be something to do with the soil, as birds generally need lime to enable them to produce shells for their eggs. But it is more probable that they happen to like one place better than another; or that they have developed the habit of living there, and that this habit persists from one generation to another. It is known, for example, that individual birds get attached to certain places when they are young, and that they often return to the place where they were originally reared, even after migrating for thousands of miles. There is still a great deal to be learnt about the distribution and dispersal of birds.

Every kind of bird has developed its own particular habits, though differences between species may be slight. It seldom happens, for instance, that two species occupying the same habitat eat exactly the same sort of food. Where they do so, you usually find that they collect it in different ways. Pelicans and cormorants both eat fish. But pelicans feed from the surface whereas cormorants dive. Fish Eagles and ospreys also eat fish, but they are birds of prey and collect their prey in a different way again. However, they themselves hunt in an almost identical manner. Fish Eagles are the more successful, and there are many more of them. The most numerous species in a habitat is usually the one which is the most successful at obtaining food; there has to be a really abundant supply of food if the less successful species is to survive.

Competition between individuals of the same species takes place in the breeding season, not only in finding a mate but also in finding somewhere to nest. Birds of two different species may also have to compete for nesting places. Often, however, where more than one species favours a particular type of cover, there is a slight difference in the height above ground at which they build their nests. Generally speaking, the more varied the habitat, the greater the variety of species which will be present.

Except in desert habitats, birds are generally more numerous in the tropics than in temperate lands. This can easily be explained by the lush conditions, which produce huge quantities of food for birds to eat, and the absence of a cold, harsh winter. There are also many more different species as we have seen already when looking at such well-known families as the flycatchers, swallows and warblers.

The continuing existence of any species depends upon the survival of individual birds, and upon their success in laying eggs and rearing their young. And this, in turn, depends upon their ability to find sufficient food, and to overcome the numerous dangers and difficulties that surround their lives.

Birds in the tropics are not threatened with extinction to quite the same extent as the larger animals. Even so, their survival depends on man, whose influence is rarely absent and is usually harmful: even in the wildest places, man lights bush-fires which destroy trees used for nesting. Changes in a habitat inevitably result in making it unsuitable for the birds which once found that it provided conditions to their liking. Birds will disappear if their surroundings and habitats are destroyed. With a growing human population and more intensive farming, this process has started already. When forests are cut down, there is nowhere for the turacos and hornbills to live.

One of the greatest threats is the indiscriminate use of poisonous insecticides on agricultural land. In parts of Europe and North America, this has already produced disastrous results as is well known. In Africa, the use of these insecticides will almost certainly spread, so that the more populous parts of the continent will soon be much less rich in bird life than they are today.

The Queen Elizabeth National Park, the Murchison Falls National Park, and other areas devoted to the conservation of wildlife, should be safe, however. They are large enough to provide permanent sanctuary for the birds. With their several different habitats, they support one of the most magnificent and varied collections of wild birds to be seen anywhere on earth.

A young Verreaux's Eagle Owl

Cattle Egret at nest

List of the Principal Birds to be found in the Uganda National Parks

(Species listed under their respective Orders, some of which have been grouped together for convenience; all sub-species have been ignored)

PELICANS AND THEIR ALLIES (six species recorded)

Cormorant	*Phalacrocorax carbo*
Long-tailed Cormorant	*Phalacrocorax africanus*
Darter or Snake Bird	*Anhinga rufa*
White Pelican	*Pelecanus onocrotalus*
Pink-backed Pelican	*Pelecanus rufescens*

HERONS, STORKS AND THIER ALLIES (32 species recorded)

Grey Heron	*Ardea cinerea*
Black-headed Heron	*Ardea melanocephala*
Goliath Heron	*Ardea goliath*
Purple Heron	*Ardea purpurea*
Great White Egret	*Casmerodius albus*
Yellow-billed Egret	*Mesophoyx intermedius*
Little Egret	*Egretta garzetta*
Buff-backed Heron or Cattle Egret	*Bubulcus ibis*
Squacco Heron	*Ardeola ralloides*
Night Heron	*Nycticorax nycticorax*
Little Bittern	*Ixobrychus minutus*
Hammerhead or Hammerkop	*Scopus umbretta*
Whale-headed Stork or Shoe-bill	*Balaeniceps rex*

HERONS, STORKS AND THEIR ALLIES (*continued*)

White Stork	*Ciconia ciconia*
Woolly-necked or Bishop Stork	*Dissoura episcopus*
Abdim's Stork	*Sphenorhynchus abdimii*
Open-bill Stork	*Anastomus lamelligerus*
Saddle-bill or Jabiru	*Ephippiorhynchus senegalensis*
Marabou Stork	*Leptoptilos crumeniferus*
Wood Ibis or Yellow-billed Stork	*Ibis ibis*
Sacred Ibis	*Threskiornis aethiopicus*
Hadada or Hagerdash Ibis	*Hagedashia hagedash*
African Spoonbill	*Platalea alba*
Greater Flamingo	*Phoenicopterus ruber*
Lesser Flamingo	*Phoeniconaias minor*

DUCKS AND GEESE (16 species recorded)

Pochard	*Aythya ferina*
African Pochard	*Aythya erythrophthalma*
Shoveler	*Spatula clypeata*
Garganey	*Anas querquedula*
Hottentot Teal	*Anas punctata*
Red-bill	*Anas erythrorhyncha*
Pintail	*Anas acuta*
White-faced Tree Duck	*Dendrocygna viduata*
Pigmy Goose	*Nettapus auritus*
Knob-billed Goose	*Sarkidiornis melanotos*
Egyptian Goose	*Alopochen aegyptiacus*
Spur-winged Goose	*Plectropterus gambensis*

BIRDS OF PREY (52 species recorded)

Secretary Bird	*Sagittarius serpentarius*
White-backed Vulture	*Pseudogyps africanus*
Lappet-faced Vulture	*Torgos tracheliotus*
White-headed Vulture	*Trigonoceps occipitalis*
Hooded Vulture	*Necrosyrtes monachus*
Peregrine Falcon	*Falco peregrinus*

Lanner Falcon	*Falco biarmicus*
Hobby	*Falco subbuteo*
Grey Kestrel	*Falco ardosiaceus*
Kite	*Milvus migrans*
Bat-eating Buzzard	*Machaerhamphus alcinus*
Tawny Eagle	*Aquila rapax*
Wahlberg's Eagle	*Aquila wahlbergi*
African Hawk Eagle	*Hieraaetus spilogaster*
Martial Eagle	*Polemaetus bellicosus*
Crowned Eagle	*Stephanoaetus coronatus*
Long-crested Hawk Eagle	*Lophoaetus occipitalis*
Short-toed Harrier Eagle	*Circaetus gallicus*
Brown Harrier Eagle	*Circaetus cinereus*
Bateleur	*Terathopius ecaudatus*
Fish Eagle	*Cuncuma vocifer*
Palm-nut Vulture	*Gypohierax angolensis*
Steppe Buzzard	*Buteo vulpinus*
Little Sparrowhawk	*Accipiter minullus*
Gabar Goshawk	*Micronisus gabar*
Dark Chanting Goshawk	*Melierax metabates*
Montagu's Harrier	*Circus pygargus*
Pallid Harrier	*Circus macrourus*
Marsh Harrier	*Circus aeruginosus*
Osprey	*Pandion haliaetus*

PHEASANT-LIKE BIRDS (12 species recorded)

Coqui Francolin	*Francolinus coqui*
Red-necked Spurfowl	*Pternistis cranchii*
Quail	*Coturnix coturnix*
Harlequin Quail	*Coturnix delegorguei*
Tufted Guinea-fowl	*Numida meleagris*
Crested Guinea-fowl	*Guttera edouardi*

CRANES, RAILS AND THEIR ALLIES (13 species recorded)

Button Quail	*Turnix nana*
Uganda Crested Crane	*Balearica regulorum*

CRANES RAILS AND THEIR ALLIES (*continued*)

Black Crake	*Limnocorax flavirostra*
African Moorhen	*Gallinula chloropus*
Finfoot	*Podica senegalensis*
Jackson's Bustard	*Neotis (denhami) jacksoni*
Black-bellied Bustard	*Lissotis melanogaster*

WADERS, GULLS AND THEIR ALLIES (56 species recorded)

Jacana or Lily-trotter	*Actophilornis africanus*
Painted Snipe	*Rostratula benghalensis*
Oystercatcher	*Haematopus ostralegus*
Ringed Plover	*Charadrius hiaticula*
Kittlitz's Sand Plover	*Charadrius pecuarius*
Three-banded Plover	*Charadrius tricollaris*
Spur-winged Plover	*Hoplopterus spinosus*
Wattled Plover	*Afribyx senegallus*
Long-toed Lapwing	*Hemiparra crassirostris*
African Snipe	*Capella nigripennis*
Curlew Sandpiper	*Calidris testacea*
Little Stint	*Calidris minuta*
Ruff	*Philomachus pugnax*
Turnstone	*Arenaria interpres*
Common Sandpiper	*Tringa hypoleucos*
Wood Sandpiper	*Tringa glareola*
Redshank	*Tringa totanus*
Dusky Spotted Redshank	*Tringa erythropus*
Marsh Sandpiper	*Tringa stagnatilis*
Greenshank	*Tringa nebularia*
Black-tailed Godwit	*Limosa limosa*
Bar-tailed Godwit	*Limosa lapponica*
Curlew	*Numenia arquata*
Avocet	*Recurvirostra avosetta*
Black-winged Stilt	*Himantopus himantopus*
Grey Phalarope	*Phalaropus fulicarius*
Water Thicknee	*Burhinus vermiculatus*

Temminck's Courser	*Cursorius temminckii*
Pratincole	*Glareola pratincola*
White-collared Pratincole	*Galachrysia nuchalis*
Lesser Black-backed Gull	*Larus fuscus*
Grey-headed Gull	*Larus cirrocephalus*
Gull-billed Tern	*Gelochelidon nilotica*
White-winged Black Tern	*Chidonias hybrida*
Scissor-billed Tern or Skimmer	*Rhynchops flavirostris*

PIGEONS AND THEIR ALLIES (14 species recorded)

Four-banded Sandgrouse	*Eremialector quadricinctus*
Mourning Dove	*Streptopelia decipiens*
Ring-necked Dove	*Streptopelia capicola*
Tambourine Dove	*Tympanistria tympanistria*
Western Lemon Dove	*Aplopelia simplex*
Green Pigeon	*Treron australis*

PARROTS (three species recorded)

Grey Parrot	*Psittacus erithacus*
Red-headed Lovebird	*Agapornis pullaria*

TURACOS, CUCKOOS AND THEIR ALLIES (18 species recorded)

Ross's Turaco	*Musophaga rossae*
Great Blue Turaco	*Corythaeola cristata*
Grey Plantain-eater	*Crinifer zonurus*
Cuckoo	*Cuculus canoraus*
Dusky Long-tailed Cuckoo	*Cercococcyx mechowi*
Emerald Cuckoo	*Chrysococcyx cupreus*
Didric Cuckoo	*Chrysococcyx caprius*
White-browed Coucal	*Centropus superciliosus*

OWLS AND NIGHTJARS (12 species recorded)

Barn Owl	*Tyto alba*
African Marsh Owl	*Asio capensis*
Verreaux's Eagle Owl	*Bubo lacteus*
Fishing Owl	*Scotopelia peli*
Nightjar	*Caprimulgus europoeus*

OWLS AND NIGHTJARS (*continued*)

Pennant-winged Nightjar	*Semeiophorus vexillarius*
Standard-winged Nightjar	*Macrodipteryx longipennis*

SWIFTS (seven species recorded)

Common Swift	*Apus apus*
Alpine Swift	*Apus melba*
Palm Swift	*Cypsiurus parvus*

MOUSEBIRDS OR COLLIES AND TROGONS (three species recorded)

Speckled Mousebird	*Colius striatus*
Narina's Trogon	*Apaloderma narina*

KINGFISHERS AND THEIR ALLIES (33 species recorded)

Pied Kingfisher	*Ceryle rudis*
Giant Kingfisher	*Megaceryle maxima*
Shining-blue Kingfisher	*Alcedo quadribrachys*
Malachite Crested Kingfisher	*Corythornis cristata*
Blue-breasted Kingfisher	*Halcyon malimbicus*
Grey-headed Kingfisher	*Halcyon leucocephala*
Bee-eater	*Merops apiaster*
Madagascar Bee-eater	*Merops superciliosus*
Carmine Bee-eater	*Merops nubicus*
Red-throated Bee-eater	*Melittophagus bulocki*
European Roller	*Coracias garrulus*
Abyssinian Roller	*Coracias abyssinica*
Broad-billed Roller	*Eurystomus glaucurus*
South African Hoopoe	*Upupa africana*
European Hoopoe	*Upupa epops*
Green Wood Hoopoe	*Phoeniculus purpureus*
Scimitar-bill	*Rhinopomastus cyanomelas*
Black and White Casqued Hornbill	*Bycanistes subcylindricus*
Grey Hornbill	*Tockus nasutus*
Crowned Hornbill	*Tockus alboterminatus*
Abyssinian Ground Hornbill	*Bucorvus abyssinicus*

WOODPECKERS AND THEIR ALLIES (16 species recorded)

Double-toothed Barbet	*Lybius bidentatus*
Lemon-rumped Tinker-bird	*Pogoniulus leucolaima*
Black-throated Honey-guide	*Indicator indicator*
Brown-eared Woodpecker	*Campethera caroli*
Little Spotted Woodpecker	*Campethera cailliautii*
Yellow-crested Woodpecker	*Mesopicos xantholophus*
Wryneck	*Jynx torquilla*

PERCHING BIRDS (208 species recorded, all except the Pitta being classed as SONG BIRDS)

African Pitta	*Pitta angolensis*
Singing Bush Lark	*Mirafra cantillans*
Flappet Lark	*Mirafra rufocinnamomea*
Swallow	*Hirundo rustica*
Red-rumped Swallow	*Hirundo daurica*
African Sand Martin	*Riparia paludicola*
African Rock Martin	*Ptyonoprogne fuligula*
White-headed Rough-wing Swallow	*Psalidoprocne albiceps*
White Wagtail	*Motacilla alba*
African Pied Wagtail	*Motacilla aguimp*
Yellow Wagtail	*Budytes flavus*
Richard's Pipit	*Anthus richardi*
Yellow-throated Long-claw	*Macronyx croceus*
Grey Cuckoo-shrike	*Coracina caesia*
Dark-capped Bulbul	*Pycnonotus xanthopyos*
Toro Olive Greenbul	*Phyllastrephus hypochloris*
Fiscal Shrike	*Lanius collaris*
Black-headed Gonolek	*Laniarius erythrogaster*
Gonolek or Red-breasted Shrike	*Laniarius barbarus*
Black-headed Bush Shrike	*Tchagra senegala*
African Thrush	*Turdus pelios*
Wheatear	*Oenanthe oenanthe*
Sooty Chat	*Myrmecocichla nigra*
White-browed Robin-chat	*Cossypha heuglini*

PERCHING BIRDS (*continued*)

Black-eared Babbler	*Turdoides melanops*
Sedge or Reed Warbler	*Acrocephalus schoenobaenus*
Willow Warbler	*Phylloscopus trochilus*
Fan-tailed Swamp Warbler	*Schoenicola brevirostris*
Green Crombec	*Sylvietta virens*
Zitting Cisticola	*Cisticola juncidis*
Spotted Flycatcher	*Muscicapa striata*
Dusky Flycatcher	*Alseonax adustus*
Wattle-eye	*Platysteira cyanea*
Paradise Flycatcher	*Tchitrea viridis*
Beautiful Sunbird	*Nectarinia pulchella*
Copper Sunbird	*Cinnyris cupreus*
Scarlet-breasted Sunbird	*Chalcomitra senegalensis*
Green White-eye	*Zosterops virens*
Golden-breasted Bunting	*Emberiza flaviventris*
Golden Oriole	*Oriolus oriolus*
Grey-headed Sparrow	*Passer griseus*
Black-headed Weaver	*Ploceus cucullatus*
Spectacled Weaver	*Hyphanturgus ocularis*
Vieillot's Black Weaver	*Melanopteryx nigerrimus*
Grosbeak Weaver	*Amblyospiza albifrons*
Red-billed Quelea	*Quelea quelea*
Fire-crowned Bishop	*Euplectes hordeacea*
Fan-tailed Widow-bird	*Coliuspasser axillaris*
Bronze Mannikin	*Spermestes cucullatus*
African Fire-finch	*Lagonosticta rubricata*
Red-billed Fire-finch	*Lagonosticta senegala*
Waxbill	*Estrilda astrild*
Purple Indigo-bird	*Hypochera ultramarina*
Pin-tailed Whydah	*Vidua macroura*
Paradise Whydah	*Steganura paradisaea*
Yellow-fronted Canary	*Serinus mozambicus*
Wattled Starling	*Creatophora cinerea*
Ruppell's Long-tailed Glossy Starling	*Lamprotornis purpuropterus*

Yellow-billed Ox-pecker	*Buphagus africanus*
Drongo	*Dicrurus adsimilis*
Piapiac	*Ptilostomus afer*
Pied Crow	*Corvus albus*
White-necked Raven	*Corvultur albicollis*

(All species mentioned in the text are included in this list together with a small number of others)

Books for Reference and Further Reading

AUSTIN, O. A. *Birds of the World* (Paul Hamblyn, 1961)

BERE, RENNIE. *Wild Animals in an African National Park* (André Deutsch, 1966)

BROWN, LESLIE. *Eagles* (Michael Joseph, 1955)

BROWN, LESLIE. *The Mystery of the Flamingoes* (Country Life, 1959)

*CAMPBELL, BRUCE. *The Oxford Book of Birds* (Oxford University Press, 1964)

DELACOUR, JEAN. *The Waterfowl of the World* (Country Life, 1954–59)

FISHER, J. and PETERSON, R. T. *The World of Birds* (Macdonald, 1964)

GÉRONDET, P. (trans. by Barclay-Smith, P.) *Water Birds with Webbed Feet* (Blandford, 1965)

LOCKLEY, R. M. *Animal Navigation* (Arthur Barker, 1967)

MACKWORTH-PRAED, C.W. and GRANT, C. H. B. *The Birds of Eastern and North-eastern Africa* (Longmans, 1952–55)

*READE, WINWOOD and HOSKING, ERIC. *Nesting Birds* (Blandford, 1967)

THOMSON, SIR A. L. (editor) *A New Dictionary of Birds* (Nelson, 1964)

WELTY, J. C. *The Life of Birds* (Constable, 1964)

WILLIAMS, J. G. *A Field Guide to the Birds of East and Central Africa* (Collins, 1965)

WILLIAMS, J. G. *A Field Guide to the National Parks of East Africa* (Collins, 1967)

*WITHERBY, H. F., JOURDAIN, F. C. R., TICEHURST, H. F., and TUCKER, B. W. *The Handbook of British Birds* (Witherby 1938–43)

(Books marked with an asterisk are relevant only in respect of Palaearctic migrants)

Index